Elaeis guineensis - New Insights

Edited by Viduranga Y. Waisundara

Published in London, United Kingdom

Elaeis guineensis - New Insights
http://dx.doi.org/10.5772/intechopen.107796
Edited by Viduranga Y. Waisundara

Contributors
Wai Onn Hong, Adeola Sarah Ajayi, Mpoko Bokanga, Flavio Linares, Viduranga Y. Waisundara, Heethaka Krishantha Sameera de Zoysa

First published in London, United Kingdom, 2024 by IntechOpen
IntechOpen is the global imprint of INTECHOPEN LIMITED, registered in England and Wales, registration number: 11086078, 5 Princes Gate Court, London, SW7 2QJ, United Kingdom
Printed in Croatia

British Library Cataloguing-in-Publication Data
A catalogue record for this book is available from the British Library

Additional hard and PDF copies can be obtained from orders@intechopen.com

Elaeis guineensis - New Insights
Edited by Viduranga Y. Waisundara
p. cm.

This title is part of the Agricultural Sciences Book Series, Volume 3
Topic: Agronomy and Horticulture
Series Editor: W. James Grichar
Topic Editor: Ibrahim Kahramanoglu
Associate Topic Editors: Murat Helvaci and Olga Panfilova

Print ISBN 978-0-85014-183-2
Online ISBN 978-0-85014-184-9
eBook (PDF) ISBN 978-0-85014-185-6
ISSN 3029-052X

For EU product safety concerns:
IN TECH d.o.o., Prolaz Marije Krucifikse Kozulić 3, 51000 Rijeka, Croatia,
info@intechopen.com or visit our website at intechopen.com.

IntechOpen Book Series

Agricultural Sciences

Volume 3

Aims and Scope of the Series

The importance of agriculture cannot be overstated. It helps sustain life, as it gives us the food we need to survive and provides opportunities for economic well-being. Agriculture helps people prosper around the world and combines the creativity, imagination, and skill involved in planting crops and raising animals with modern production methods and new technologies. This series includes two main topics: Agronomy and Horticulture, and Animal Farming. This series will help readers better understand the intricacies of production agriculture and provide the new knowledge that is required to be successful. The success of a farmer in modern agriculture requires knowledge of events happening locally as well as globally that impact input decisions and ultimately determine net profit.

Meet the Series Editor

W. James Grichar has been employed with Texas A&M AgriLife Research for over 45 years with an emphasis on research in agronomy, plant pathology, and weed science. He obtained his BS from Texas A&M in 1972 and his Masters of Plant Protection in 1975. He has published 195 journal articles, over 330 research reports and briefs, 11 book chapters, and over 300 abstracts of profession meetings. He also directs research in many crops including corn, grain sorghum, peanuts, and sesame. He has held various positions in different professional societies including the American Peanut Research and Education Society, Southern Weed Science Society, and Texas Plant Protection Conference in addition to being Associate Editor for Peanut Science and Weed Technology. Significant accomplishments have included spearheading efforts to determine the optimum planting time for soybean production along the upper Texas Gulf Coast. These efforts have shown growers that soybean yields can be improved by 10 to 20% by following a late March to early April plant date. He also has been instrumental in developing a herbicide program for peanut production in the south Texas growing region. Through the development and use of herbicides that are effective against major weed problems in the south Texas region, peanut yields have increased by 25 to 30%.

Meet the Volume Editor

Dr. Viduranga Waisundara obtained her Ph.D. in Food Science and Technology from the Department of Chemistry, National University of Singapore in 2010. She was a lecturer at Temasek Polytechnic, Singapore from July 2009 to March 2013. She relocated to her motherland of Sri Lanka and spearheaded the Functional Food Product Development Project at the National Institute of Fundamental Studies from April 2013 to October 2016. She was a senior lecturer on a temporary basis at the Department of Food Technology, Faculty of Technology, Rajarata University of Sri Lanka. She is currently Deputy Principal of the Australian College of Business & Technology – Kandy, Sri Lanka. She is also the current Global Harmonization Initiative (GHI) Ambassador to Sri Lanka.

Contents

Preface

The oil palm industry is one of the most historically important commercial businesses. Oil palms were introduced to Java by the Dutch in 1848 and to Malaysia in 1910 by Scotsman William Sime and English banker Henry Darby. *Elaeis guineensis* was taken to Malaysia from Eastern Nigeria in 1961. However, it originally grew in West Africa. Oil is extracted from both the pulp of the fruit and the kernel.

The high oil yield of oil palms has made it a common cooking ingredient in Southeast Asia and tropical Africa. Its increasing use in the commercial food industry in other parts of the world is due to its low cost. *E. guineensis* is among the few tropical tree crops with high productivity in actual growing conditions.

This book discusses the technologies involved in the palm oil industry as well as the processes and procedures involved, while investigating and focusing on methods aimed at conserving its sustainability. The book consists of two sections that include chapters written by experts who have provided a detailed overview of the industry as well as insights on maintaining sustainability. The chapter authors come from varied backgrounds, exposures, and location, and therefore, look at the oil palm industry from multiple perspectives, leading to the book's holistic overview of the global palm oil industry.

I would like to take this opportunity to extend my appreciation to the authors who have contributed so many wonderful chapters. Also, my heartfelt appreciation goes to IntechOpen with whom I have worked on many book projects. Finally, my appreciation goes to the Publishing Process Manager Ms. Ana Javor, who provided unfailing support in throughout the publication process.

I hope that this book will lay the foundations for many more publications to come on *E. guineensis*. There is much to be learned and discovered about the palm oil industry and its future will be successful if challenges are dealt with appropriately and overcome.

Dr. Viduranga Y. Waisundara
Deputy Principal,
Australian College of Business and Technology,
Kandy Campus, Kandy, Sri Lanka

Section 1

Basic Overview of *Elaeis guineensis* and the Industry

Chapter 1

Introductory Chapter: *Elaeis guineensis* – An Overview and an Update

Heethaka Krishantha Sameera de Zoysa and Viduranga Y. Waisundara

1. Introduction

Elaeis guineensis is a species of palm that is commonly known as oil palm; it may sometimes be known as African oil palm or macaw-fat as well [1]. Being native to West and Southwest Africa, it is the principal source of palm oil for the African continent. The species is also now naturalized in Madagascar, Sri Lanka, Malaysia, Indonesia, Central America, Cambodia, West Indies, and several islands in the Indian and Pacific Oceans [2].

The palm fruit takes approximately 6 months to develop from pollination to maturity. It is red in color and grows in large bunches. Each fruit is made up of an oily, fleshy pericarp, with a single seed (the palm kernel), which is also rich in oil.

1.1 Background

Palm oil is extracted from both the pulp of the fruit (palm oil, which is an edible oil) and the kernel (palm kernel oil, which is used in foods and for soap manufacture). The high yield of palm oil has made it a cooking ingredient in Southeast Asia, Africa, and various other parts of the world as well. Its increasing use in the commercial food industry in other parts of the world is due to cost efficiency, high oxidative stability, and the presence of antioxidants [3].

1.2 Significance of *Elaeis guineensis* in agriculture

Elaeis guineensis, beyond economic value, plays a vital role in addressing water scarcity in agriculture. Climate change poses challenges to oil palm cultivation, affecting land suitability and economic stability. Understanding soil properties, moisture parameters, and adopting sustainable practices are essential for navigating these complex dynamics [4]. The significance of *E. guineensis* extends to sustainable agricultural practices, as it impacts the management of water resources, soil properties, and the complex relationship between climate change and oil palm cultivation. Moreover, the multifaceted uses of oil palm make it a valuable and versatile crop with profound implications for agriculture, environment, and society at large. As global demand for palm oil is expected to double by 2050, it is imperative to consider the sustainable

IntechOpen

management of *E. guineensis* to ensure a balance between agricultural productivity and environmental conservation [4, 5].

Climate change is expected to reshape the suitability of locations for oil palm plantations in the twenty-first century, making a substantial portion of current cultivation areas unsuitable due to rising temperatures and increased droughts. This will particularly impact countries such as Thailand, Colombia, Nigeria, Indonesia, and Malaysia. Despite potential adaptations, such as elevational shifts, they are unlikely to fully compensate for the loss of suitable cultivation areas. Malaysia, a significant player in the oil palm industry, faces considerable economic and livelihood consequences. This intricate relationship between climate and soil dynamics underscores the need for a comprehensive understanding of the multifaceted impacts of climate change on the oil palm industry, as climate plays a major role in the formation and development of soil, including its texture and the soil organic matter cycle [4, 6]. Nevertheless, innovative approaches, such as the use of biofertilizers, have gained attention in oil palm plantations. Biofertilizers, which contain beneficial microorganisms, enhance soil microbial activity and offer a cost-effective and eco-friendly alternative to chemical fertilizers. These microorganisms not only promote plant growth but also reduce the need for inorganic fertilizers, contributing to sustainable farming practices [7].

Furthermore, agricultural waste generated from *E. guineensis* has proven valuable in the production of pharmaceutical-grade activated charcoal. The unique surface morphology and pore structure of this activated charcoal enhances its adsorption capabilities, making it a promising material for medical and industrial applications, such as biofuel production. It offers a sustainable and eco-friendly solution, utilizing agricultural waste to create valuable resources [8, 9]. Overall, the oil palm holds an insightful significance in agriculture, impacting soil management, water resources, climate change adaptation, and sustainable practices. Its versatile uses and innovative approaches in its cultivation underscore its importance in the agricultural landscape, offering solutions to pressing global challenges.

2. Origins and global distribution

Oil palm holds a significant interest in terms of its origins and global distribution. This tropical perennial plant, a member of the Arecaceae family, is native to the coastal regions of the Gulf of Guinea in West and Central Africa, displaying a unique "temporally dioecious" reproductive pattern. Historical findings dating back to 3000 BC in an Egyptian tomb in West Africa suggest the utilization of palm oil for over 5000 years, with the species introduced to the Americas during the sixteenth century. It was not until 1940 that its formal cultivation began in Honduras and Costa Rica, leading to its establishment in Ecuador, Guatemala, Venezuela, Peru, and Mexico. As a crucial source of edible oil from its fruit mesocarp and kernels, oil palm serves as a vital dietary component globally, with its by-products finding diverse applications in various industries. Predominantly, Indonesia, Malaysia, and Thailand in Southeast Asia lead in oil palm cultivation, contributing to 88% of the world's total fruit yield, with smaller yet notable contributions from Colombia and Nigeria. The origins of oil palm trace back to West and Central Africa, along the Atlantic Coast, spreading from Cape Verde to Angola and extending inland into parts of Congo-K and Congo-B. Early trade routes facilitated the distribution of oil palm from West Africa to regions as distant as East Tanzania and islands such as Pemba, Zanzibar, and Madagascar. The primary oil palm-growing countries include

Angola, Benin, Cameroon, Congo, Ghana, Cote d'Ivoire, Ivory Coast, Nigeria, Sierra Leone, Brazil, Colombia, Costa Rica, Ecuador, Indonesia, Malaysia, Papua New Guinea, and Thailand. Indonesia and Malaysia dominate global production, contributing 81% of the total fruit yield. Global palm oil production has significantly increased, covering an extensive area of 17 million hectares, with India cultivating oil palm across 11 states, primarily led by Andhra Pradesh. Various factors, including genetic resources, environmental conditions, and cultural practices, influence oil yield, with oil palms displaying adaptability to diverse environments. Soil compaction minimally affects fresh fruit bunch yield, and ongoing research into oil palm nutrition and production technologies continues to shape the industry, particularly with the development of new breeds and genetic makeup uniformity [10–12].

2.1 Role as a major agricultural crop

Today, oil palm remains central to human consumption, supplying essential edible oil derived from its fruit mesocarp and kernels. This crop extends its value beyond the culinary world, as its by-products play crucial roles in the food, cosmetic, chemical, and biofuel industries, making it a versatile and economically attractive commodity. The majority of oil palm cultivation now thrives in Southeast Asia, specifically in Indonesia, Malaysia, and Thailand, accounting for 81% of the world's total fruit yield, with additional contributions from countries such as Colombia and Nigeria. The global oil palm production has significantly increased, spanning approximately 17 million hectares. In India, oil palm is now cultivated across 11 states, with Andhra Pradesh holding a prominent position. It's essential to understand that various factors influence oil yields, such as genetic resources, environmental conditions (humidity, water availability, and soil texture), and cultural practices. The future of oil palm lies in ongoing research to develop new breeds with uniform genetic makeup, advanced production technologies, and an ever-growing global demand due to its diverse applications across industries [9, 10, 12].

3. Palm oil production and trade

Palm oil production and trade are integral components of the global economy, particularly in regions like Southeast Asia. Oil palm, a perennial monocotyledonous plant, is the primary source of palm oil, a valuable commodity with diverse applications [13]. The significance of palm oil in the global economy is exemplified by Indonesia's substantial contribution. Indonesia's palm oil-related businesses have been instrumental in the country's economic development, contributing significantly to its GDP and foreign exchange revenue. The Crude Palm Oil (CPO) by-product of the *E. guineensis* tree plays a central role in this economic growth. Not only does the palm oil industry provide employment to over 16 million people, but it also enhances social welfare through innovative programs like the nucleus-plasma model, fostering partnerships between plantation companies and local communities. This dynamic sector has witnessed tremendous growth, with Indonesia surpassing Malaysia as the world's largest CPO producer. Presently, Indonesia dominates the global CPO production, accounting for over 60% of the total production, with Malaysia as the second largest producer. The demand for CPO is on the rise, driven by various industries, including food, biofuels, oleochemicals, and stearin, making it a cornerstone of Indonesia's economic landscape. However, the industry faces environmental challenges, especially concerning deforestation, which has raised concerns about biodiversity loss. These challenges underscore the need for sustainable practices and environmental conservation within the palm oil sector [14, 15].

Palm oil production and trade play a pivotal role not only in economic growth but also in shaping the environmental and social landscape of producing countries. Addressing issues such as seed dormancy and sustainable cultivation practices is vital to ensure the continued prosperity of the palm oil industry while minimizing its impact on the environment. The global demand for palm oil remains significant, underscoring the importance of effective and responsible management in this critical sector.

3.1 Overview of palm oil production worldwide

Palm oil production is a crucial industry with global significance, primarily driven by the cultivation of *Elaeis guineensis*, the high-yielding species native to West Africa. This valuable crop found its way to Southeast Asia, specifically Indonesia and Malaysia, during the nineteenth century, where it quickly evolved into a major economic force. Malaysia, in particular, has embraced oil palm cultivation, and by 2020, it stood as one of the world's largest producers. The global palm oil industry now boasts a staggering worth of approximately US$60 billion. Currently, these two countries account for approximately 84% of the world's total oil palm cultivation. The significance of this industry is further underscored by the fact that oil palm is the highest produced vegetable oil globally, outstripping soybean and rapeseed oils. As demand for palm oil increases, driven by its widespread use in cooking and various consumer products across Africa and Asia, production is anticipated to continue its upward trajectory. Estimates suggest that as the global population expands, palm oil production will soar to between 93 and 156 million tons by 2050 [4, 5, 13, 15].

3.2 Dominant producers: Malaysia and Indonesia

Oil palm cultivation is predominantly concentrated in equatorial tropical regions, with 42 countries worldwide engaging in its growth. Key players in this industry are Indonesia and Malaysia, which together contribute a significant 84% to the global output. Malaysia, in particular, stands as the world's second largest oil palm producer after Indonesia, with the sector contributing a substantial 37.7% of revenues to the country's agricultural sector in 2019. The economic importance of palm oil cannot be overstated, and its continued growth is critical to these countries' prosperity. Oil palm's versatility, high yield per unit of land, and profitability have solidified its place as a major global oil crop. It is used in a wide range of products, from cooking oil to cosmetics and biodiesel. Malaysia and Indonesia, as the world's top producers, play a pivotal role in meeting global palm oil demand. However, climate change and environmental concerns may impact Malaysia's oil palm output in the future. Nevertheless, the palm oil industry continues to thrive, offering significant economic benefits and a reliable source of vegetable oil and biofuels for the world [4, 7, 13, 15].

Despite its economic potential, oil palm cultivation has not been without controversy. Its expansion has led to large-scale land conversion, particularly in Southeast Asian peatlands, resulting in significant carbon emissions [4]. Sustainable management and environmental considerations are vital aspects of the industry's future, especially in Malaysia and Indonesia, where large-scale peatland conversions have occurred. Stricter regulations and better practices are needed to address the environmental impact while still harnessing the economic potential of palm oil [4].

3.3 Global significance in edible oil production and trade

The global significance of palm oil in the realm of edible oil production and trade is of paramount importance, especially as the world anticipates a substantial population increase by 2050. The intricate process of palm oil production begins with the collection of crude oil extracted from the sterilized mesocarp and kernel. This crude oil undergoes rigorous refining stages, including bleaching and deodorization, resulting in the creation of highly refined oils that find application both independently and in combination with other cooking oils, salad dressings, and margarines. Beyond the realm of culinary use, palm oil's reach extends further through a fractionalization process that yields olein and stearin, alongside the extraction of valuable fatty acids and alcohols. These derivative products play a pivotal role in the food and oleochemical industries, encompassing applications in cosmetics, packaging, and a myriad of other sectors. The versatility and ubiquity of palm oil underscore its indispensability in global trade, rendering it a highly sought-after commodity. The escalating demand for palm oil extends beyond the final product and encompasses the germinated seeds essential for cultivating oil palm trees. As the industry continues to grow, a steady supply of these seeds becomes imperative. In essence, palm oil serves as the linchpin of global edible oil production and trade, addressing the world's ever-expanding dietary and industrial requirements while remaining a versatile and indispensable component of the global economy [4, 5, 13].

4. Objectives of the book

The purpose of this book is to provide scientific and nonscientific audiences alike with an overview of the palm oil industry, processing, by-products, needs, and opportunities. Not just the African palm oil industry, the book provides insights into the practices all around the world. It is hoped that the contents of the book will provide new knowledge and information, and elucidate best practices since the environmental impact of the palm oil industry is a matter of concern and debate around the world.

Author details

Heethaka Krishantha Sameera de Zoysa[1] and Viduranga Y. Waisundara[2*]

1 Faculty of Technology, Department of Bioprocess Technology, Rajarata University of Sri Lanka, Mihintale, Sri Lanka

2 Australian College of Business and Technology – Kandy Campus, Kandy, Sri Lanka

*Address all correspondence to: viduranga@gmail.com

References

[1] Okolo CC, Okolo EF, Nnadi AL, Obikwelu FE, Obalum SE, Igwe CA. The oil palm (*Elaeis guineensis Jacq*): nature's ecological endowment to eastern Nigeria. Agro-Science Journal of Tropical Agriculture, Food, Environment and Extension. African Journals OnLine (AJOL). 2019;**18**(3):48-57. DOI: 10.4314/as.v18i3.9

[2] Purugganan MD, Fuller DQ. The nature of selection during plant domestication. Nature. Nature Research. 2009;**457**(7231):843-848

[3] Che Man YB, Liu JL, Jamilah B, Rahman RA. Quality changes of RBD palm olein, soybean oil and their blends during deep-fat frying. Journal of Food Lipids. 1999;**6**(3):181-193

[4] McCalmont J, Kho LK, Teh YA, Chocholek M, Rumpang E, Rowland L, et al. Oil palm (*Elaeis guineensis*) plantation on tropical peatland in South East Asia: Photosynthetic response to soil drainage level for mitigation of soil carbon emissions. Science of the Total Environment. 2023;**858**:1-13. DOI: 10.1016/J.SCITOTENV.2022.159356

[5] Unnikrishnan J. Systematic Analysis of Reproductive Development in Normal and Mantled Oil Palm (*Elaeis guineensis* Jacq) Flowers and Fruit. Malaysia: University of Nottingham; 2023

[6] Abubakar A, Ishak MY, Bakar AA, Uddin MK, Ahmad MH, Seman IA, et al. Geospatial simulation and mapping of climate suitability for oil palm (*Elaeis guineensis*) production in peninsular Malaysia using GIS/remote sensing techniques and analytic hierarchy process. Modeling Earth Systems and Environment. 2023;**9**(1):73-96. DOI: 10.1007/S40808-022-01465-9/FIGURES/7

[7] Peng SHT, Chee KH, Saud HM, Yusop MR, Tan GH. Potential novel plant growth promoting rhizobacteria for bio-organic fertilizer production in the oil palm (*Elaeis guineensis* Jacq.) in Malaysia. Applied Sciences, Page 7105. 2023;**13**(12):1-16. DOI: 10.3390/APP13127105

[8] Ilomuanya M, Nashiru B, Ifudu N, Igwilo C. Effect of pore size and morphology of activated charcoal prepared from midribs of *Elaeis guineensis* on adsorption of poisons using metronidazole and *Escherichia coli* O157:H7 as a case study. Journal of Microscopy and Ultrastructure. 2017;**5**(1):32-38. DOI: 10.1016/J.JMAU.2016.05.001

[9] Okonkwo CP, Ajiwe VIE, Ikeuba AI, Emori W, Okwu MO, Ayogu JI. Production and performance evaluation of biodiesel from *Elaeis guineensis* using natural snail shell-based heterogeneous catalyst: Kinetics, modeling and optimisation by artificial neural network. RSC Advances. 2023;**13**(28):19495-19507. DOI: 10.1039/D3RA02456C

[10] Magaña-Álvarez A, Pérez-Brito D, Cortés-VelázquezA,Nexticapan-GarcézÁ, Ortega-Ramírez ME, García-Cámara I, et al. Genetic variability of oil palm in Mexico: An assessment based on microsatellite markers. Agriculture. 2023;**13**(9):1-12. DOI: 10.3390/AGRICULTURE13091772/S1

[11] Mihai RA, Melo Heras EJ, Landazuri Abarca PA, Catana RD. The fungal, nutritional, and metabolomic diagnostics of the oil palm *Elaeis guineensis* affected by bud rot disease in Esmeraldas,

Ecuador. Journal of Fungi, Page 952. 2023;**9**(9):1-17. DOI: 10.3390/JOF9090952

[12] Murugesan P, Aswathy GM, Kumar KS, Masilamani P, Kumar V, Ravi V. Oil palm (*Elaeis guineensis*) genetic resources for abiotic stress tolerance: A review. Indian Journal of Agricultural Sciences. 2017;**87**(5):571-579. DOI: 10.56093/ijas.v87i5.70087

[13] Nadarajah UM, Hazirah I, Nawi M. Heat treatment application on oil palm seed—a review. Tropical Agriculture. 2023;**100**(2):127-135. Available from: https://journals.sta.uwi.edu/ojs/index.php/ta/article/view/8439

[14] Limaho H, Sugiarto S, Pramono R, Christiawan R. The strategy of palm oil plantation expansion business in relation to environmental sustainability issues: Overcoming the challenges. Eduvest—Journal of Universal Studies. 2023;**3**(5):1007-1018. DOI: 10.59188/EDUVEST.V3I5.820

[15] Rao MCS, Rao BN, Swami DV, Ashok P, Ramani GR, Rao BB, et al. Management and processing of palm oil (*Elaeis guineensis* Jacq): The crop for future. In: Waisundara VY, editor. Palm Oil - Current Status and Updates. London, UK: IntechOpen; 2023. pp. 1-17. DOI: 10.5772/INTECHOPEN.108579

Chapter 2

Advances in Sustainable Palm Oil Milling Technologies: Enhancing Efficiency and Environmental Performance

Wai Onn Hong

Abstract

This chapter conducts a thorough examination of current and emerging palm oil milling technologies, emphasizing their role in enhancing efficiency while addressing environmental concerns. Structured into four sections, it begins by evaluating traditional milling methods and equipment, considering their effectiveness and environmental impact in sterilization, threshing, digestion, and oil clarification. The subsequent section explores cutting-edge advancements, including automation and biotechnology applications for improved efficiency and resource optimization. The third section focuses on initiatives to reduce carbon emissions, highlighting technologies for enhanced energy efficiency, renewable energy integration, and improved waste management. Lastly, the chapter delves into the concept of a circular economy in the palm oil industry, emphasizing waste reduction, resource optimization, and sustainable practices throughout the palm oil production process. It discusses biomass utilization, by-product valorization, and integrated palm oil biorefineries as essential elements of circular economy approaches. This comprehensive exploration aims to familiarize readers with *Elaeis guineensis* and advocate for a more sustainable future in the palm oil industry, providing a thorough understanding of contemporary milling technologies and their potential to mitigate environmental impact.

Keywords: palm oil industry, palm oil milling, oil extraction, renewable energy, carbon footprint, circular economy, biotechnology

1. Introduction

Palm oil, derived from the fruit of the oil palm tree, is a globally consumed and widely traded edible vegetable oil. The palm oil industry has undergone remarkable expansion, primarily driven by factors, such as the rapid growth of the global population and increased per capita consumption. Consequently, global palm oil production has experienced substantial growth, surging from 24 million tons (t) in 2000–2001 to an impressive 78 million t in 2021–2022 [1]. Projections further suggest that palm oil production is set to reach 156 million tons by 2050, underscoring its pivotal role in meeting escalating global demand.

The surge in palm oil production has solidified its position in the global oils and fats market, owing to its affordability, versatility, and unique properties. Palm oil finds applications across various industries, including food, nonfood, and bioenergy. Its exceptional heat stability renders it an ideal choice for frying applications. Its neutral flavor and diverse fat compositions have made it a preferred ingredient in packaged baked goods, snacks, and margarine. Furthermore, palm oil's natural absence of trans-fats positions it as a healthier option for consumers. Trans fats, commonly present in partially hydrogenated vegetable oils, are frequently used in processed foods to enhance texture and shelf life. Moreover, palm oil extends its use to nonfood applications such as soaps, detergents, and cosmetics, given its ability to create a stable lather and offer moisturizing properties. In addition to this, palm oil holds promise as a renewable energy source within the bioenergy sector, where its cost-effective raw material contributes to biofuel production.

Indonesia and Malaysia emerge as key players in the global palm oil landscape, serving as primary producers with extensive oil palm plantations and well-established palm oil milling facilities. Presently, Indonesia stands as the world's leading palm oil producer, accounting for approximately 60% of total production, followed by Malaysia at around 25% [1]. Beyond these two giants, several other nations significantly contribute to the global palm oil industry, including Thailand, Colombia, Nigeria, and Papua New Guinea.

The palm oil value chain comprises distinct segments (**Figure 1**), commencing with the upstream sector involving activities such as oil palm plantation, palm oil milling, and kernel crushing plants. Further down the supply chain, the midstream processing facilities include palm oil refineries. The downstream segment encompasses specialty fats, oleochemical, and biodiesel producers [2]. While the entire value chain holds relevance, this chapter's primary focus lies on palm oil milling.

The subsequent sections of this chapter will delve into sustainable palm oil milling technologies, addressing their role in enhancing efficiency and minimizing the environmental footprint of the milling process. This exploration encompasses a

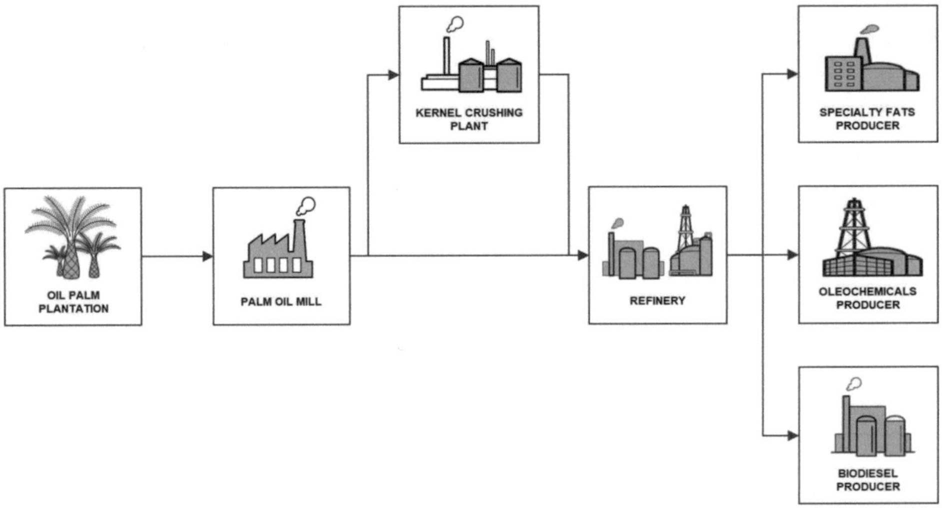

Figure 1.
Palm oil processing value chain. Created by Wai Onn Hong, 2020.

comprehensive assessment of both traditional methods and equipment, an examination of the latest advancements in automation and biotechnology, initiatives aimed at reducing carbon emissions, and the incorporation of circular economy principles within the palm oil industry.

2. Palm oil milling operations

The typical palm oil milling process flow is best described through a series of activities conducted in different stations (**Figure 2**). It all begins with the transportation of fresh fruit bunches (FFB) from plantation sites to the palm oil mills. The milling operation includes several stages, namely reception, sterilization, threshing, digestion and pressing, clarification and purification, and kernel recovery. The primary products obtained from these processes are crude palm oil and palm kernels, while several forms of biomass are generated, including pressed mesocarp fibers, palm kernel shells, empty fruit bunches, and decanter solids. The liquid waste byproduct, called palm oil mill effluent, is a combination of various waste streams such as sterilizer condensate, heavy phase from clarification, and wastewater from wet separation. Within a palm oil mill, a power plant is also present, comprising a boiler house and an engine room that generates steam to drive steam turbines, producing power. The exhaust steam from the turbine serves to facilitate various processes within the mill.

2.1 Reception and sterilization

FFB delivered to the palm oil mill undergo inspection and grading for ripeness and quality standards before being loaded onto ramp hoppers and cages. These cages are transported into a horizontal sterilizer and subjected to steam heating at 143°C and 3 bar gauge pressure for approximately 90 minutes, in a process known as sterilization [3]. This procedure deactivates hydrolytic enzymes, eases the separation of individual fruits from bunches, and prepares the nuts for subsequent processing by reducing kernel breakage during pressing and nut cracking.

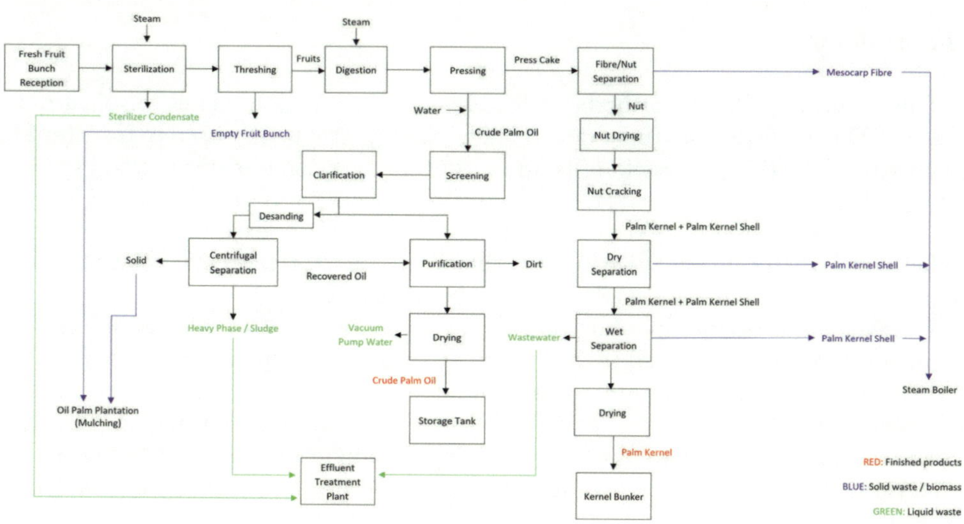

Figure 2.
Typical palm oil milling process. Created by Wai Onn Hong, 2020.

Parameter	Horizontal batch sterilizer	Vertical batch sterilizer	Continuous sterilizer
Operation mode	Batch	Batch	Continuous
Sterilization method	Steam and bunches in cages	Steam and bunches in a vessel	Steam and bunches on a conveyor
Sterilization pressure	Medium	Medium	Atmospheric pressure
Sterilization time	Moderate	Moderate	High
FFB movement	FFB cages	Conveyor system	Conveyor system
Labor requirement	Manual or automated operation	Automated operation	Automated operation
Space requirement	High	Moderate	Low
Environmental impact	Energy intensive	Energy intensive	Energy-efficient
Oil losses	Low to moderate	Moderate to high	Low to moderate

Table 1.
Contrasting horizontal batch sterilizer, vertical batch sterilizer, and continuous sterilizer.

Various types of sterilizers are commonly used in palm oil mills, including horizontal batch sterilizers, vertical batch sterilizers, and continuous sterilizers. Each type has specific characteristics that influence its operation, although the fundamental principles remain consistent (**Table 1**). Additionally, there are other less common sterilizers such as tilting, oblique, spherical, and multidoor system horizontal kinetic sterilizers, with only minor variations from the three primary sterilizer types.

Notably, the sterilization process results in the production of a byproduct referred to as sterilizer condensate. This condensate constitutes a blend of water and a medley of compounds liberated from the fruits during the sterilization phase. Rather than being cycled back into the production line, there is an increasing emphasis on the management and potential reutilization of this condensate. These endeavors have acquired significant relevance as palm oil mills seek to enhance their environmental performance through sustainable practices.

2.2 Threshing

There are two primary methods for feeding sterilized fruit bunches (SFB) into the thresher. The overhead hoisting crane or cage tipper is frequently used to transfer SFB from cages to the thresher in oil mills. In mills utilizing a cageless sterilization system, a scrapper conveyor is employed to consistently transport SFB to the thresher. The first method involves lifting, tipping, and rotating cages to release SFB onto an auto feeder, which then conveys them into the thresher. The latter method uses a series of chain conveyors to move SFB to the thresher continuously.

The thresher is essentially a horizontal rotating drum. SFB is loaded at one end, lifted, and repeatedly dropped as they travel through the drum, which rotates at about 22 rotations per minute. This process is designed to separate palm fruits from bunch stalks and typically incorporates a double-stage threshing approach. This approach aims to minimize unstripped bunches, ensuring the highest possible oil and kernel extraction rates. After passing through the first-stage thresher, SFB will typically undergo a second-stage threshing step to further minimize the presence of unstripped bunches. In some cases, roller crusher machines are used to loosen partially unstripped bunches after the initial stage of threshing.

Detached palm fruits pass through bar screens in the drum and are then conveyed to a digester, while the remaining bunch stalks, also known as empty fruit bunches, are used for mulching in plantations. In certain oil mills, additional processing is employed on these empty fruit bunches. They are shredded and subjected to pressing, resulting in two distinct products: empty fruit bunch liquor and empty fruit bunch fibers. The empty fruit bunch liquor can be marketed as secondary oil or technical-grade oil, while the empty fruit bunch fibers become a valuable solid fuel resource for the steam boiler. This dual utilization underscores the resource efficiency within palm oil mills.

2.3 Digestion and pressing

The digestion and pressing stations represent the core of the palm oil milling process, where palm oil is extracted from the fruits. Fruitlets, which have undergone sterilization, are conveyed to vertical cylindrical digesters where they are heated by steam and mashed by stirring arms. This process serves to loosen the mesocarp from the nuts and break open oil-bearing cells to release the crude oil. Proper digestion of the fruitlets typically requires a residence time of 30 minutes [4]. The digested mash is then fed into a continuous screw press that extracts the oil-containing liquor, leaving behind press cake, composed of pressed mesocarp fibers and nuts.

Advancements in the design of screw presses have led to the use of single or double screw pressing systems. Double screw pressing is especially effective in maximizing oil extraction while minimizing nut breakage. The capacity of screw presses has also increased, reducing the number of units required for milling operations. These screw presses now have design capacities ranging from 3 to 4 to 25–30 tonnes of FFB per hour. However, it is essential to ensure that any capacity upgrade of the screw press is accompanied by an increased digester capacity to prevent a shortened residence time in the digester, which could result in ineffective digestion of fruitlets.

2.4 Clarification and purification

The press liquor extracted during the pressing stage contains a mixture of palm oil, water, and solid or fibrous materials. This mixture is diluted with water and passed through a vibrating screen to remove coarse contaminants before being transferred to a crude oil tank, which serves as a rectangular buffer tank. Crude oil is then subjected to clarification at temperatures ranging from 90 to 95°C in a vertical settling tank or clarifier tank, where gravity separation takes place [5].

Improvements in the design of crude oil tanks have included the installation of coalescence plates, which enhance the oil separation process by reducing the droplet settling distance. With these enhancements, millers can initiate oil harvesting at this stage, as opposed to the traditional process where oil harvesting occurs at a later point. The underflow from the crude oil tank is then further clarified in another vertical settling tank.

In the vertical settling tank, oil, being the lighter phase, is skimmed from the top and subjected to a high-speed centrifugal purifier to remove any remaining impurities. Afterward, it is transferred to a vacuum dryer to reduce moisture. The final product, crude palm oil, is pumped into a storage tank before being sent to refineries for further processing.

The heavier phase or underflow from the vertical settling tank, often referred to as sludge, is discharged from the bottom and directed to a sludge tank before

Parameter	Star-bowl centrifuge	Nozzle separator	Three-phase decanter
Separation principle	Centrifugal force	Centrifugal force	Centrifugal force
Oil recovery	Efficient	Efficient	Efficient
Capacity and throughput	Moderate	Low to moderate	High
Cleaning requirement	Moderate	Moderate	Low
Space requirement	Moderate	Low	Moderate
Capital investment cost	Low	Moderate	High

Table 2.
Contrasting star-bowl centrifuge, nozzle separator, and three-phase decanter.

undergoing desanding. It then enters a centrifugal separator, such as a star-bowl centrifuge, nozzle separator, or three-phase decanter, to recover any remaining oil (**Table 2**). The water and fibrous debris or heavy phase generated are discharged as palm oil mill effluent.

Although it is common practice to dilute the press liquor with hot water, some oil mills operate an oil recovery system without dilution. In this system, the press liquor is processed without the use of a vertical settling tank, instead relying on a specially designed two-phase decanter. This approach significantly reduces the volume of liquid by-products generated, leading to a reduced environmental impact.

2.5 Kernel recovery

The press cake, a tightly compressed mass produced during pressing, is fragmented in a cake breaker conveyor to loosen its structure and reduce its moisture content. Subsequently, it goes through a pneumatic separation process to effectively separate the nuts from the pressed mesocarp fibers.

The nuts are further polished in a polishing drum to remove and separate any remaining fibers from the nuts. This step is crucial for the efficiency of the nut-cracking process, which is essential for obtaining palm kernels and palm kernel shells. Excessive fibers attached to the nuts create a cushioning effect that hampers the cracking process.

The separation of palm kernels and palm kernel shells is achieved through a multi-stage winnowing system, which includes dry separation followed by clay bath, hydro-cyclone wet separation, or a combination of both. Palm kernels are subsequently dried and stored, ready to be dispatched to kernel crushing plants. Palm kernel shells and pressed mesocarp fibers find utility as solid fuel feedstock for the steam boiler.

2.6 Boiler station

Palm oil mills are typically self-sufficient in energy generation due to the ample availability of biomass. The steam boiler within the boiler station is responsible for producing steam, which, in turn, drives a steam turbine to generate power and facilitates various processes such as sterilization, digestion, and clarification. Steam boiler operation can be simplified as the presence of "a hot heat-transfer surface covered with water." This heat-transfer surface generates steam bubbles that rise through the water and enter the steam system. The steam can leave the boiler in either superheated form or in a saturated state, depends on the boiler's specific design.

The process of steam generation has evolved from less efficient and labor-intensive small-capacity fiber tube boilers to automated water tube boilers. These advanced systems feature components like a "walking floor" boiler fuel storage system, moving grates for fuel combustion, and an ash removal system.

2.7 Engine room

The engine room serves as a station for generating electrical energy, utilizing both diesel generator sets and steam turbines to power a palm oil mill and its associated housing complex.

During the operation of a palm oil mill, steam turbines are relied upon for electricity generation. However, steam pressure fluctuations can occur, sometimes falling below the required level. In such cases, the diesel generator set is activated to reduce the load on the turbine.

Traditionally, diesel generator sets were the sole source of electricity during non-processing hours. Nevertheless, recent advancements have enabled many palm oil mills to operate their steam boilers and generate electricity even when the mill is not actively processing. This is achieved through automation in the fuel feeding system, allowing continuous fuel feed from stored reserves even during non-processing hours.

3. Progressive improvements in palm oil milling

The palm oil milling industry, deeply rooted in tradition, has undergone a remarkable transformation in recent years. This evolution has brought substantial enhancements to the traditional thermo-mechanical milling process, making it not only more efficient but also safer and environmentally sustainable. These advancements in efficiency and sustainability are the fruits of a deliberate integration of cutting-edge computational power, machine learning, automation systems, and innovative biotechnological solutions.

In the upcoming section, we will embark on a comprehensive journey to explore the multifaceted improvements that have been the driving force behind the palm oil milling industry's progressive transition toward enhanced sustainability and resource efficiency.

3.1 The data-driven transformation of palm oil milling

In recent years, the palm oil milling industry has been quick to harness the significant surge in available computing power, which has led to substantial improvements in data analysis. This transformation has not only made the analytical process more cost-effective but also substantially more efficient. Companies operating within the industry have been swift to recognize the enormous potential of this enhanced computational capacity. By integrating data analysis and machine learning, they are initiating a profound shift in the way they conduct business, ultimately revolutionizing their approach to planning and process efficiency [6].

For instance, palm oil companies are now capable of leveraging historical production data to predict optimal processing times, enabling them to streamline their operations with pinpoint accuracy. This amalgamation of data analysis offers the potential to unlock heightened operational efficiency while concurrently reducing waste. It plays a crucial role in advancing the overall sustainability of the palm oil milling sector.

3.2 Machine learning's role in enhancing milling efficiency

Spectral imaging, a well-proven technology recognized for its ability to evaluate the internal quality characteristics of diverse fruits, has undergone recent trials in the palm oil milling industry. This innovative application entails the use of spectral imaging to assess the quality of FFB as they are delivered to the mills. This marks a significant advancement, as it offers an essential initial evaluation of FFB quality, laying the foundation for subsequent milling processes that are not only more efficient but also more precise.

To enhance this evaluation, machine learning algorithms have been employed [7]. These advanced algorithms are designed to analyze the spectral data obtained from the FFB, enabling the accurate assessment of each fruit bunch's quality. These insights serve as the foundation for creating intelligent systems that can autonomously categorize FFB based on their quality. The implementation of such systems is a pivotal step toward streamlining the milling operation. For instance, these intelligent systems can automatically segregate low-quality FFB, ensuring that only those meeting specified quality standards are subjected to further processing.

One of the most significant advantages of this approach is the ability to adjust sterilization parameters in response to the quality of the FFB. This adaptability ensures that each batch of FFB is subjected to precisely tailored sterilization processes, thus preventing the common issues of under steaming or over steaming. By doing so, the overall efficiency of the milling operation is substantially enhanced, leading to a reduction in process losses. This dual effect, characterized by increased efficiency and minimized wastage, represents a significant stride in the quest for more sustainable and resource-efficient palm oil milling practices.

3.3 Automation across various milling stations

Automation has permeated the sterilization process, revolutionizing the traditional manual procedures. Steam admission into pressure vessels is now contingent on properly closed doors, and these doors cannot be opened if the vessel remains pressurized. This technological advancement not only mitigates potential safety hazards but also leads to the prevention of unwarranted accidents. Furthermore, the implementation of advanced steam management system in sterilization station ensures a precise and efficient steam supply, catering to the varying quality of fresh fruit bunches, all the while preventing steam wastage and safeguarding against excessive steam extraction from the boiler.

The influence of automation reaches far beyond the sterilization phase. It has sparked pivotal transformations across various milling stations, generating notable improvements in safety, operational efficiency, and overall sustainability. One prominent transition includes the widespread replacement of capstan and bollard systems with hydraulic indexing systems. This shift not only minimizes the risk of accidents that could result from workers being wedged between fresh fruit bunch cages but also significantly reduces the industry's dependence on manual labor.

Moreover, the transition from conventional hoisting crane systems to modern tipper systems has introduced heightened safety measures for operators. This change is particularly crucial for safeguarding the well-being of workers who might be exposed to risks caused by issues such as chain or wire sling failures, defective rings, eye bolts, and shackles, which can be prone to defects, overloading, corrosion, or excessive wear and tear. Notably, this transition has eliminated the occurrence of accidents, such as three-tonne cage failures from great heights due to system failures, which were not uncommon in the past.

In the digestion station, advanced automation systems are effectively maintaining the optimal quantity of fruitlets in the digester. This ensures that the digestion process runs with peak efficiency before the fruitlets are discharged to the screw press. The application of automation in the press station is equally noteworthy, where it plays a pivotal role in achieving the dual objectives of maximizing oil extraction and minimizing nut breakage. These automated processes not only enhance overall productivity but also contribute to the industry's drive toward sustainability and resource optimization.

Although automation is already widely implemented in the clarification station, there is still considerable potential for further enhancement in oil skimming process, with the aim of reducing labor dependency. For example, the introduction of automated oil skimming mechanisms utilizing state-of-the-art technologies, such as time-domain reflectometry, can be explored in the vertical settling tank. By accurately pinpointing the interface between oil and sludge, this automation has the capacity to fine-tune oil skimming with exceptional precision [7]. This innovation not only serves to diminish the industry's reliance on manual labor but also guarantees consistent optimization of the clarification processes, thereby mitigating the risks associated with under- or over-skimming in the vertical settling tank.

The adoption of automation in the kernel recovery station is another significant development. In this context, automation systems govern the heating and discharge sequences within kernel silos. This precision control ensures that kernels undergo optimal drying before they are transferred to the kernel bunker for storage. Additionally, this automation contributes to reducing the risk of fire incidents in the kernel recovery station by eliminating the possibility of overheating. These advancements in automation reflect a commitment to both operational efficiency and safety, reinforcing the palm oil milling sector's efforts to align with sustainable and environmentally responsible practices.

3.4 Revolutionizing palm oil milling through enzymatic biotechnology

Traditionally, palm oil milling processes involved sterilization and digestion to facilitate mechanical oil extraction. However, this method has reached its limits, evident from the stagnant oil extraction rates over the years. The introduction of enzymatic biotechnology, a significant breakthrough in the palm oil industry, holds the promise of overcoming this challenge. Enzymes, with their ability to break down plant cell walls effectively, could revolutionize oil release and substantially enhance extraction efficiency.

Enzymatic processes, requiring minimal steps and reasonable investments, promise remarkable improvements to the bottom line. By effectively breaking down the cell walls of palm fruit, enzymes boost oil extraction efficiency without compromising the quality of crude palm oil. Several palm oil companies have either experimented with or fully adopted enzymatic biotechnology, resulting in a noteworthy increase in oil production [8, 9]. This breakthrough not only ensures enhanced efficiency but also markedly reduces the industry's environmental footprint associated with land use, a pivotal stride toward sustainable practices.

4. Reducing carbon emissions in palm oil milling

The palm oil industry, frequently under the scrutiny of environmental critics, has embarked on a profound transformation aimed at achieving higher levels of sustainability. Central to this transformation is a concerted drive to reduce carbon emissions. The palm oil industry recognizes the pivotal role it plays in the broader context of environmental conservation and climate change mitigation. This recognition has catalyzed a dynamic shift toward more sustainable practices and technologies, ushering in an era, where carbon emissions are no longer an inevitable consequence of palm oil production. In their relentless pursuit of emission reduction, palm oil companies are at the forefront of pioneering groundbreaking approaches that span across the entirety of palm oil milling operations.

This section unravels the notable advancements in the industry's quest for sustainability. In stark contrast to other oil crop processing facilities, palm oil mills stand out as pioneers of energy self-sufficiency, distancing themselves from conventional power sources, such as grid electricity and fuel oil. Moreover, this section discusses biogas utilization, showcasing the capture of methane emissions for electricity generation and its potential for wider applications, including bio-compressed natural gas. The section concludes by recognizing palm sludge oil as a biodiesel feedstock, emphasizing its environmental benefits, potential for reducing carbon emissions, and its alignment with sustainability and energy demands.

4.1 Self-sufficient energy practices in palm oil mills

In contrast to other oil crop processing facilities, palm oil mills have established themselves as environmentally conscious entities, pioneering a sustainable approach to energy generation. These mills have eschewed reliance on conventional energy sources, such as electricity from the national grid and fuel oil. Instead, they have long been on a path toward sustainability, leading the industry in achieving energy self-sufficiency by harnessing the potential of biomass resources. These resources include pressed mesocarp fibers, palm kernel shells, and empty fruit bunch fibers, which are expertly utilized in cutting-edge cogeneration facilities.

This concerted effort to tap into renewable energy sources has far-reaching implications not only for the palm oil milling sector but for the broader environmental landscape. Energy consumption in the milling process is no small matter, with estimates pegging it at around 18.7 kilowatt-hours per tonne of fresh fruit bunch processed [10]. This is a substantial energy demand, especially considering that the combined production of the world's top two palm oil producers, Indonesia and Malaysia, amounted to approximately 287 million tonnes of fresh fruit bunches in 2022.

The significance of cogeneration systems in achieving energy self-sufficiency cannot be overstated. These systems have ushered in a new era of sustainability and environmental responsibility. By relying on their self-sufficient design, Indonesia and Malaysia have jointly achieved a momentous feat—significantly reducing carbon emissions. To put this achievement into perspective, it amounts to a remarkable 2500 thousand metric tons of carbon dioxide (CO_2) emissions saved.

Such a feat is not merely a commendable accomplishment in the field of carbon avoidance; it is also a resounding contribution to the global fight against climate change. The palm oil milling sector's commitment to energy self-sufficiency stands as a pivotal step in preserving our environment, underscoring its significance in addressing the overarching issue of global warming. This journey toward sustainability in the palm oil industry showcases a path that others can follow, one that leads to not only operational efficiency but also environmental responsibility.

4.2 Harnessing biogas for sustainability

Palm oil mills produce large quantities of palm oil mill effluent (POME), which has long been recognized as a significant contributor to global climate change. This is because POME naturally decomposes in the absence of oxygen, producing biogas, primarily composed of methane. Methane is a potent greenhouse gas, with a global warming potential (GWP) 25 times greater than that of carbon dioxide [11]. If biogas emissions are not effectively controlled, methane is released directly into the atmosphere. However, the silver lining lies in the fact that this biogas simultaneously represents a valuable renewable energy source, offering the prospect of a sustainable solution.

Palm oil mills have embarked on a transformative journey toward achieving a net-zero carbon footprint. Central to this transition is the capture and conversion of biogas, mitigating methane emissions while concurrently generating renewable energy. This paradigm shift revolves around utilizing biogas for electricity generation, primarily through gas turbines. The electricity generated has two uses: it can power the mill, and in some situations, extra power can be sent to the national grid, benefiting nearby homes through the Feed-in-Tariff scheme. By adopting this environmentally responsible approach, palm oil mills not only prevent methane emissions into the atmosphere but also contribute to the generation of green energy.

Indeed, the potential applications of the biogas generated in palm oil mills extend beyond electricity generation. This versatile resource can be directed into multiple avenues, offering avenues for sustainability. One path involves feeding the biogas directly into the steam boiler system, where it serves as an efficient and eco-friendly fuel source. This not only reduces the mills' reliance on fossil fuels during non-processing hours but also enhances their self-sufficiency in energy production. Furthermore, biogas can undergo an upgrading process to become bio-compressed natural gas (Bio-CNG), a clean and sustainable alternative to traditional fossil fuels. By taking this approach, palm oil mills can further reduce their environmental footprint and participate in the broader goal of transitioning to eco-friendly energy sources.

While biogas power plants are not uncommon in palm oil plantations, their full potential has not yet been realized. The primary obstacle lies in the associated costs of constructing biogas plants, substations, and high-tension lines, particularly in the rural areas, where palm oil mills are typically located. Nevertheless, the palm oil industry's proactive stance in fully harnessing this renewable energy source will not only contribute significantly to reducing carbon emissions but also provide an affordable, reliable, sustainable, and modern energy source for rural communities. The time has come to unlock the true potential of biogas and reshape the landscape of both palm oil production and rural energy accessibility.

4.3 Palm sludge oil as a sustainable biodiesel feedstock

During the production of crude palm oil, a liquid by-product, palm oil mill effluent (POME), is generated. Instead of being left in the effluent treatment pond, palm sludge oil, a common term used to describe residual oil from POME, could become an attractive natural source for biodiesel production.

Biodiesel, produced from different triglyceride sources, is an alternative petrodiesel fuel. To date, refined palm oil has been one of the most common biodiesel feedstock type. However, the biodiesel industry has been under pressure due to rising concerns about feedstock availability and pricing. As a result, affordable and lower-quality oils like POME oil are becoming a hopeful choice for making biodiesel. This aligns with the increasing need for eco-friendly energy sources, moving away from using food-based materials for biodiesel production. Remarkably, POME oil exhibits a commendable environmental profile, boasting zero life cycle greenhouse gas emissions up to the point of its collection. The significance of this feedstock extends to the point where it qualifies for double accounting of greenhouse gas savings under the renewable energy directive, as recognized by the International Sustainability and Carbon Certification [12].

The transition to POME oil-based biodiesel not only underscores the environmental stewardship of palm oil companies but also positions them as significant contributors to global carbon reduction efforts.

5. Circular economy principles in palm oil

The palm oil industry holds the potential to not only advance technologically but also to explore innovative business models. Embracing the principles of the circular economy, which are centered on the reduction of waste and the maximization of resource efficiency in both product and process design, can offer a promising pathway. By adopting these principles, the industry can efficiently harness agricultural biomass, promote resource conservation, and unlock new avenues for business development.

In an era, where the imperative of sustainability reigns supreme, industries globally are undergoing a paradigm shift in their resource management and waste reduction practices. A frontrunner in this movement is the palm oil sector, a crucial player in the global food and bioenergy supply chain. As sustainability continues to take center stage, the integration of circular economy principles into palm oil manufacturing and waste management surfaces as a potent strategy to curtail environmental impact and fortify overall sustainability.

The concept of the circular economy model paints a vivid picture of a regenerative system, meticulously designed to maximize resource efficiency, minimize waste generation, and extend product lifecycles through thoughtful design, reuse, and recycling. This model represents a significant departure from the traditional linear approach of "take-make-dispose" and has been steadily gaining traction across various industrial domains. The impetus behind this transformation is the aspiration to disentangle economic growth from resource depletion and environmental degradation.

The palm oil industry, which has been under scrutiny for its environmental footprint, now stands at a pivotal juncture, poised for a transformation guided by the principles of the circular economy. This section extensively explores the plausible incorporation of circular economy principles across diverse domains within palm oil production, presenting avenues for enhanced resource efficiency and a substantial reduction in waste generation. In embracing these practices, the industry not only addresses its sustainability issues but also positions itself as a potential pioneer in sustainable and responsible resource stewardship.

5.1 Transforming waste into resources

The concept of circularity within the palm oil milling industry hinges on the efficient and resourceful management of valuable assets, effectively reframing waste as a valuable resource rather than a disposal concern. A standout example of this circular paradigm is the creative repurposing of organic waste, notably empty fruit bunches (EFB), which undergo transformation into natural mulch and are reintroduced into the fields. This circular system yields a plethora of benefits, encompassing its role in efficient weed control, the mitigation of soil erosion, the preservation of soil moisture, and, notably, the substantial reduction in waste disposal, marking a significant stride toward environmental responsibility.

Furthermore, POME emerges as an untapped resource reservoir. Its application in field irrigation, especially during prolonged dry spells, proves invaluable in alleviating moisture stress on oil palms. Beyond its role as an irrigation source, when POME is distributed across the fields, it acts as a supplementary nutrient source, enhancing the overall health and productivity of oil palms. This dual-pronged approach to repurposing organic waste is not merely an exercise in waste minimization; it embodies a comprehensive resource optimization strategy in line with the fundamental tenets of a circular economy.

Adding depth to this sustainable cycle, the co-composting of EFB and POME results in the creation of nutrient-rich organic fertilizer [13]. This integration of organic materials into the agricultural cycle fundamentally elevates soil fertility, ultimately cultivating the growth of robust and productive palm plantations.

5.2 Second-generation bioethanol from palm oil biomass

Another notable transformation within the palm oil industry involves the strategic utilization of palm oil biomass, encompassing various components, including oil palm trunk, oil palm fronds, empty fruit bunches, and palm kernel cake. These diverse biomass sources serve as rich reservoirs of cellulosic biomass, holding the potential for significant environmental and economic benefits. The process begins with a crucial pre-treatment step, where cellulosic biomass is broken down into pulp. After this, the cellulose and hemicellulose components, which form the structural framework of these biomaterials, are efficiently hydrolyzed into simpler sugars.

This hydrolysis process sets the stage for the subsequent step, where yeasts come into play, adeptly fermenting these simple sugars to produce second-generation bioethanol. The remarkable similarity to first-generation bioethanol production is seen in the subsequent separation of ethanol from the fermentation broth through the distillation process. However, the environmental and performance benefits of second-generation bioethanol are notably distinct. The advantages of this sustainable fuel source are multifaceted. Notably, it carries the potential to reduce greenhouse gas emissions by over 80% when compared to conventional gasoline [14], marking a significant stride in combating climate change and reducing carbon footprints. Furthermore, second-generation bioethanol boasts a higher-octane number [15], an attribute that not only aligns with environmental sustainability but also enhances engine performance. This transformative approach in the palm oil industry showcases how sustainable practices and innovation can go hand in hand, resulting in both ecological and industrial benefits.

5.3 From palm kernel cake to poultry feed

Palm kernel cake (PKC), a residual product derived from the extraction of palm kernel oil, has traditionally found use as dairy cattle feed due to its protein, fat, and energy content. However, its adoption in poultry diets has been limited, primarily because of its high fiber content. Nonetheless, a pioneering biotechnological solution offers the prospect of expanding its applications. When PKC is directed into bioethanol production, it gives rise to a valuable by-product known as distiller's dried grains with solubles (DDGS). This nutrient-rich DDGS material is a residue resulting from the yeast fermentation process and exhibits the potential to replace traditional corn and soybean meals in broiler diets without compromising performance [16, 17].

In Indonesia and Malaysia, where broiler meat is a dietary staple, substantial quantities of soybean meal, approximately 6.7 million tonnes in 2021, are imported for the poultry industry [18]. By optimizing the use of all PKC generated in these countries, it is anticipated that this can significantly offset a substantial portion, potentially up to 70%, of imported soybean meal. Although no specific environmental study has been conducted in this regard, researchers have noted that DDGS-based diets in other industries tend to have a lower carbon footprint compared to conventional corn-soybean meal diets. The transformation of PKC into a protein-rich animal feed not only promotes the efficient utilization of agricultural biomass but also aligns with broader societal objectives related to climate mitigation and sustainability. This innovative approach not only bolsters the utilization of a valuable agricultural resource but also contributes to our collective efforts in addressing climate-related challenges.

5.4 Palm oil biomass in the bioplastic revolution

The petrochemical industry has witnessed the rapid expansion of petroleum-based plastics, making it the fastest-growing material sector over the past several decades. Notably, it is projected that plastics will contribute to 20% of total oil consumption by the year 2050 [19], underscoring the pressing need for eco-friendly alternatives to mitigate emissions.

Palm oil biomass offers a promising avenue for addressing this issue. The enzymatic hydrolysis of cellulosic biomass results in the production of simple sugars, which can serve as sustainable building blocks for various applications, including the production of bio-based monoethylene glycol (MEG). MEG, a key component in polyethylene terephthalate (PET), finds extensive use in a wide range of products, with plastic beverage bottles being one of the most common applications [20]. Although traditional sources for bio-based MEG have primarily consisted of hardwood feedstocks obtained from sawmills and by-products of the wood industry [21], evidence supports the feasibility of transitioning to palm oil biomass as a source for green chemistry [22]. This illustrates the transformative potential of palm oil biomass in revolutionizing the bioplastic market and steering it toward greater sustainability.

6. Conclusion

In conclusion, this chapter provides a comprehensive overview of the contemporary landscape of palm oil milling technologies and their pivotal role in elevating efficiency while mitigating environmental implications. The four main sections of this chapter have collectively shed light on the transformation occurring within the palm oil industry from traditional practices to cutting-edge advancements. The first section examined conventional palm oil milling techniques, evaluating their effectiveness and environmental impact. The second section delved into innovative technologies and practices, emphasizing data analysis, machine learning, automation, and biotechnology applications as drivers of efficiency and resource optimization. The third section highlighted the industry's efforts to reduce carbon emissions through self-sufficient energy practices, biogas harnessing, and the utilization of palm sludge oil as a sustainable biodiesel feedstock. The fourth section introduced the concept of a circular economy in palm oil milling, showcasing the potential of biomass utilization, by-product valorization, and integrated palm oil biorefineries to minimize waste and optimize resources.

These insights serve to acquaint readers with the dynamic landscape of *Elaeis guineensis*, emphasizing a commitment to a more sustainable future within the palm oil industry. By embracing contemporary milling technologies and integrating sustainability practices, the industry can proactively address environmental concerns while maintaining efficient production. It is our hope that this chapter has not only informed but also inspired stakeholders within the palm oil sector to embark on a path toward enhanced efficiency, lower environmental impact, and a more sustainable and responsible future. As the industry continues to evolve, these advances in sustainable palm oil milling technologies will play a pivotal role in its transformation and environmental stewardship.

Author details

Wai Onn Hong
WE ACT Services Sdn Bhd, Jalan Prima Tropika, Taman Prima Tropika, Selangor, Malaysia

*Address all correspondence to: hongwaionn@gmail.com

References

[1] USDA Economics, Statistics and Market Information System. 2023. Available from: https://usda.library.cornell.edu/concern/publications/tx31qh68h?locale=en#release-items [Accessed: August 18, 2023]

[2] Onn HW. A Chemical Engineer in the Palm Oil Milling Industry. Malaysia: Hong Wai Onn; 2021. p. 34. Available from: https://www.google.com.my/books/edition/_/4lfuDwAAQBAJ?hl=en&sa=X&ved=2ahUKEwj61fHGyuOCAxXvTmwGHfQFDLgQ8fIDegQIChAE

[3] Maycook JH. Palm Oil Factory Process Handbook Part 1, General Description of the Palm Oil Milling Process. Malaysia: Palm Oil Research Institute of Malaysia; 1985. pp. 17-30. Available from: https://books.google.com.my/books/about/Palm_Oil_Factory_Process_Handbook_Part_1.html?id=Wxl2wgEACAAJ&redir_esc=y

[4] Maycook JH. Palm Oil Factory Process Handbook Part 1, General Description of the Palm Oil Milling Process. Malaysia: Palm Oil Research Institute of Malaysia; 1985. pp. 33-38. Available from: https://books.google.com.my/books/about/Palm_Oil_Factory_Process_Handbook_Part_1.html?id=Wxl2wgEACAAJ&redir_esc=y

[5] Maycook JH. Palm Oil Factory Process Handbook Part 1, General Description of the Palm Oil Milling Process. Malaysia: Palm Oil Research Institute of Malaysia; 1985. pp. 57-74. Available from: https://books.google.com.my/books/about/Palm_Oil_Factory_Process_Handbook_Part_1.html?id=Wxl2wgEACAAJ&redir_esc=y

[6] Foong SZY, Andiappan V, Tan R, Ng DKS. Optimization and analysis for palm oil mill operations via input-output optimization model. EDP Sciences. 2019;**206**:1-6. DOI: 10.1051/matecconf/201926802006

[7] Goh SH. Malaysian oil science and technology: Malaysian oil scientists' and technologists'. Association. 2021;**30**(2):154-158

[8] Oils & Fats International Magazine. 2018. Available from: https://www.ofimagazine.com/content-images/news/Enzymes.pdf [Accessed: September 18, 2023]

[9] Silvamany H et al. Engineering Solutions for the Palm Mill of the Future: Increasing Extraction Rate and Sustainability through Biotechnology. Malaysia, United Kingdown: IOP Conference Series: Materials Science and Engineering; 2021. DOI: 10.1088/1757-899X/1195/1/012061

[10] Onn HW. Review on carbon footprint of the palm oil industry: Insights into recent developments. IJSDP. 2023;**18**(2):447-455. DOI: 10.18280/ijsdp.180213

[11] United States Environmental Protection Agency. 2023. Available from: https://www.epa.gov/gmi/importance-methane#:~:text=Methane%20is%20the%20second%20most,trapping%20heat%20in%20the%20atmosphere [Accessed: September 18, 2023]

[12] The International Sustainability & Carbon Certification. 2022. Available from: https://www.iscc-system.org/wp-content/uploads/2022/08/ISCC_Guidance_WR_from_Palm_Oil_Mills_V3.0.pdf [Accessed: September 28, 2023]

[13] The International Sustainability & Carbon Certification. 2015. Available

from https://www.youtube.com/watch?v=wrQUTES9wQY [Accessed: October 08, 2023]

[14] United States Department of Energy. 2008. Available from: https://www.energy.gov/articles/biofuels-greenhouse-gas-emissions-myths-versus-facts [Accessed: October 08, 2023]

[15] United States Department of Energy. 2023. Available from: https://afdc.energy.gov/fuels/ethanol_fuel_basics.html [Accessed: October 08, 2023]

[16] Food and Agriculture Organization. 2014. Available from: https://www.fao.org/3/i3650e/i3650e.pdf [Accessed: October 08, 20232]

[17] Alshelmani MI, Abdalla EA, Kaka U, Basit MA. Nontraditional feedstuffs as an alternative in poultry feed. In: Patra AK, editor. Advances in Poultry Nutrition Research. 3rd ed. London, UK: IntechOpen; 2021. DOI: 10.5772/intechopen.95946

[18] IndexMundi. 2023. Available from: https://www.indexmundi.com/agriculture/?commodity=soybean-meal&graph=imports [Accessed: October 08, 2023]

[19] World Economic Forum. 2016. Available from: https://www3.weforum.org/docs/WEF_The_New_Plastics_Economy.pdf [Accessed: October 08, 2023]

[20] Onn HW. Biological solutions: Catalyst for the sustainability transition of the palm oil industry. BJSTR. 2022;**47**(4):39705-38710. DOI: 10.26717/BJSTR.2022.47.007531

[21] UPM Chemicals. 2023. Available from: https://www.upm.com/businesses/upm-biochemicals/ [Accessed: October 23, 2023]

[22] Forbes. 2022. Available from: https://www.forbes.com/sites/petronas/2022/02/01/leveraging-technology-to-drive-sustainability/?sh=70c2b88f4cac [Accessed: October 23, 2023]

Section 2

Palm Oil Sustainability

Chapter 3

Utilizing Waste Derived from *Elaeis guineensis* (African Oil Palm) for Partial Cement Replacement in Stabilizing Compressed Earth Blocks

Adeola Sarah Ajayi

Abstract

The increasing demand for sustainable construction practices necessitates innovative approaches to reduce the environmental impact of conventional building materials like cement. African oil palm waste, abundant in palm-producing regions, represents a promising alternative material. This research explores the feasibility of utilizing waste materials derived from *Elaeis guineensis* (African oil palm) as a partial cement replacement in the stabilization of compressed earth blocks (CEBs). This study involves the collection and preparation of shells from oil palm waste for use in compressed earth block (CEB) production. Various proportions of these waste materials are mixed with conventional soil and cement to assess their impact on CEB properties. Compressive strength, durability, and environmental considerations are key parameters evaluated in this investigation. Preliminary findings suggest that incorporating oil palm waste in CEBs can enhance their compressive strength and reduce the carbon footprint associated with cement production. Moreover, this approach has the potential to address waste management issues in palm oil-producing regions while promoting sustainable construction practices. The research contributes to the development of eco-friendly building materials and aligns with global efforts to mitigate the environmental impact of the construction industry.

Keywords: *Elaeis guineensis*, African oil palm waste, cement replacement, compressed stabilized earth blocks, sustainable construction, waste utilization, environmental sustainability

1. Introduction

In the pursuit of sustainable and environmentally conscious construction practices, researchers and practitioners have increasingly turned their attention to innovative solutions that minimize resource depletion and waste generation. This chapter delves into a promising avenue within this realm by investigating the potential utilization of waste derived from *Elaeis guineensis*, commonly known as the African oil palm. The focus here lies in its application as a partial replacement for cement in the stabilization of compressed earth blocks (CEBs). This approach holds the promise of addressing two critical concerns simultaneously: the responsible disposal of agricultural waste and the enhancement of earth-based construction techniques.

The urgency of sustainable construction practices cannot be overstated. Traditional building methods often rely heavily on resource-intensive materials such as cement, contributing significantly to carbon emissions and depleting finite natural resources. In this context, exploring alternative materials that not only curtail these detrimental impacts but also harness agricultural waste is of paramount importance. *Elaeis guineensis*, a tree widely cultivated in various tropical regions for its oil-rich fruit, has emerged as a focal point for such exploration.

The utilization of waste derived from *Elaeis guineensis* presents a unique opportunity to transform a potential environmental burden into a valuable resource. The African oil palm industry generates substantial quantities of waste, including empty fruit bunches, palm kernel shells, and fibers. These by-products, if not managed properly, can contribute to pollution and environmental degradation. However, they also possess characteristics that make them potentially suitable for various applications, including construction materials.

Compressed Earth Blocks (CEBs) offer a sustainable and low-carbon alternative to conventional bricks or concrete blocks. By stabilizing the soil with cement, lime, or other binders, CEBs provide durability and strength while minimizing the need for resource-intensive materials. This chapter investigates the viability of incorporating waste from *Elaeis guineensis* into the binder matrix of CEBs, thus serving a dual purpose of enhancing the blocks' properties and diverting agricultural waste from landfills or open burning.

The multifaceted benefits of this approach extend beyond waste management and resource conservation. The use of agricultural waste in construction materials can contribute to rural economic development by creating new markets for these materials and promoting sustainable practices within the agricultural sector. Additionally, by reducing the reliance on cement, which is a significant contributor to greenhouse gas emissions during its production, this innovative solution aligns with global efforts to mitigate climate change.

As we delve deeper into this chapter, we will explore the mechanical and environmental aspects of incorporating *Elaeis guineensis* waste into CEBs. Through a combination of experimental analysis and theoretical considerations, we aim to provide a comprehensive understanding of the potential advantages, challenges, and considerations associated with this sustainable construction approach. By shedding light on the practicality and effectiveness of utilizing waste from the African oil palm in earth-based construction, we hope to contribute to the ongoing dialog surrounding environmentally conscious building practices and inspire further research and adoption of innovative solutions in the field.

2. African oil palm and its waste

Approximately three decades ago, the global production of oil palm experienced a nearly threefold increase. By the period of 2009–2010, the anticipated worldwide output of palm oil was projected to reach 45.1 million tons. Notably, Malaysia and Indonesia collectively contributed 85% to this production, each yielding more than

18 million tons. A report from the United Nations Economic and Social Commission for Asia and the Pacific (UN ESCAP) identified Indonesia and Malaysia as the principal contributors to the substantial presence of oil palm residues in Southeast Asian nations.

The extraction of oil from fresh fruit bunches leads to the generation of liquid and solid by-products, including fiber, shell, and seepage. Consequently, issues pertaining to pollution of the air, rivers, oceans, and groundwater have escalated due to the disposal of these waste materials. The responsible and effective management of agricultural by-products becomes imperative for the advancement of sustainable practices.

To mitigate environmental pollution stemming from oil palm cultivation, the principle of the "zero waste policy" must be extended to by-products. This entails utilizing empty fruit fibers for fuel and employing the ash as fertilizer. Historically, waste derived from the shells of African Oil Palm, more commonly known as Palm Kernel Shells (PKS), has been inadequately managed and often discarded near mills. Research indicates that PKS aggregates possess an abrasion value of approximately 4.8%, along with significantly lower impact and crushing values compared to conventional crushed stone aggregates. Consequently, PKS exhibits potential as a construction by-product.

Recent developments have seen the incorporation of palm kernel shells in the construction of access roads for oil palm mills. However, there is a paucity of published reports regarding their performance. Palm Kernel Shells (PKS) are acquired through the crushing or threshing of palm fruit to extract palm seeds subsequent to palm kernel oil extraction. Significant volumes of palm kernel shells are produced in Ondo State and Edo State, Nigeria, with moderate quantities available in other regions, particularly in the South.

Due to their inherent hardness, PKS demonstrates resilience once integrated into concrete, thereby minimizing the release of contaminants or toxic substances. Furthermore, PKS obviates the need for the processing of artificial aggregates or industrial by-products before their application, a distinction from certain artificially manufactured aggregates and industrial by-products.

The process of oil extraction at the mill industry generates both liquid wastes and solid residues. The endocarps of palm kernel shells (PKS), due to their sturdiness and hardness, fulfill the role of safeguarding palm kernels, which exhibit considerable variation in size and shape. With their natural lightweight characteristics, these shells offer a potential alternative for coarse aggregates in lightweight construction applications. Their intrinsic hardness and organic composition render them suitable for integration into concrete production, and their matrix-like structure minimizes the likelihood of contaminant release or formation of harmful substances. Notably, PKS-based lightweight concrete presents advantages over aerated concrete, as it exhibits lower permeability and reduced susceptibility to carbonation.

Palm kernel shells display an irregular shape after cracking, lacking a distinct and uniform definition. The cracks on the shells exhibit a range of forms, including semi-circular, parabolic, uneven, and flaking. While the overall contour of the shell demonstrates convex and concave features, the edges become coarse and spiky upon cracking. The thickness of the shell is found to vary, contingent upon the originating species, typically falling within the range of 2 to 3 millimeters.

Numerous studies have incorporated PKS as aggregate in concrete production, resulting in notable transformations in lightweight concrete (LWC) structures. Notably resilient, the shells resist deterioration even after being submerged for

24 hours, with water absorption capacity increasing by 21 to 33%. In comparison with conventional gravel aggregates, PKS displays higher water absorption capabilities. When incorporated into an accurately formulated mix design, PKS can effectively enhance the properties of concrete with an average strength of 20 to 30 MPa. In contrast, limited research has explored the potential of PKS for masonry purposes, particularly as bricks.

Over time, the construction of sustainable housing in numerous developing countries has frequently relied on clay mud. This housing approach is particularly favored by individuals with moderate to low incomes. The current landscape of housing development poses a significant challenge due to the substantial financial investments it demands. Additionally, when considering environmental factors, the feasibility of utilizing industrial waste in infrastructure development becomes apparent, given that these materials adhere to established standards and specifications. Efforts are being directed toward identifying alternative applications for industrial by-products, rather than allowing them to decay unused. The exploration of environmentally friendly material recycling and energy conservation has gained prominence in recent decades. Conversely, the surge in environmental regulations has heightened the demand for eco-friendly materials within the construction sector. A continuous investigation is imperative to ascertain the potential of palm kernel shells (PKS) for the production of masonry blocks. It is viable to partially replace traditional aggregates with PKS in the creation of sand-concrete blocks.

Wastes originating from the oil palm industry are often discarded without any profitable utilization, resulting in adverse environmental impacts. PKS encompasses particles of varying sizes: 0–5 mm, 5–10 mm, and 10–15 mm. In addition to posing challenges for disposal and waste management, these shells lack commercial value. The integration of palm kernel shells into construction practices is not prevalent in Ghana; local blacksmiths employ them as fuel, and they can serve as fillers or palliatives.

2.1 Applications of palm kernel shells

Various palm species, such as Dura, Pisifera, and Tenera, exhibit distinctions in their shells, fibrous oily components, and fruits primarily attributed to differences in thickness. Specifically, the Dura type is characterized by a slim fibrous component and an extensively thick shell. In contrast, the Pisifera variety typically possesses a minute shell or none at all, largely due to its fibrous nature, resulting in limited or negligible kernel production. The Tenera species combines attributes of both Dura and Pisifera, featuring a moderately thick shell and a medium-sized fiber component.

Palm kernel shells are put to the following uses:

i. Essential as a significant fuel source for domestic cooking in various regions.

ii. Generally treated as waste materials within the oil industry and subsequently discarded.

iii. Employed by blacksmiths and goldsmiths to create bellows for the purpose of iron/gold melting.

iv. Potential for producing terrazzo materials using palm kernel shells.

v. In some areas, utilized to fill potholes within muddy terrain.

vi. Possibility of generating pre-stressed concrete through lightweight aggregates derived from shells, offering valuable thermal insulation.

3. Incorporating African oil palm shell ash (palm kernel shell ash) for earth block stabilization

Compressed earth blocks (CEBs), commonly referred to as compressed stabilized earth blocks (CSEBs), encompass compact brick elements with well-defined properties, obtained by compacting soil within a wet mold and promptly demolding. The cohesion of CEBs is influenced by the clay content within the soil. CSEBs, a refined variant of CEBs, are augmented through the inclusion of additives. As CEBs are sensitive to water, additives are introduced to counteract this effect. These additives not only address color and shrinkage cracks but can also modify other attributes. Additionally, CSEBs can be known as stabilized soil blocks (SSBs), Stabiblocs, Terracretes, Soilcretes, or Pressed Soil Blocks (PSBs).

Modern CSEBs evolved from molded soil blocks, also known as adobe blocks. Initial iterations of CSEBs employed wooden tamps, elevating the quality of molded earth blocks. Although the concept of enhancing strength through soil compression is not novel, the development of motor-driven, mechanical, and manual compactors in the 1970s and 1980s facilitated the emergence of the compressed earth block industry. Earth is the oldest building material, yet its popularity waned with the advent of modern construction materials and techniques until the energy crisis prompted its resurgence. Growing environmental concerns have further spurred the utilization of soil as a global building material.

CSEBs offer numerous advantages over alternative building materials [1]:

i. It leverages local materials, reducing transportation expenses and fostering local economic activity.

ii. Construction is swifter and requires less skilled labor, yielding stronger, better-insulated, and thermally efficient structures.

iii. Waste levels are minimal, and disposal is straightforward.

iv. Environmental pollution is negligible.

v. Energy efficiency and eco-friendliness, reducing energy use and emissions. The production phase generates fewer carbon emissions and lower embodied energy.

vi. Local production, reducing costs and promoting sustainability.

vii. Durability against harsh weather conditions when properly designed and constructed.

viii. Mitigation of deforestation, as CSEB production does not require firewood.

ix. Adaptability to diverse technical, esthetic, cultural, and social needs.

x. Transferable technology that is easy to learn and requires semi-skilled labor.

xi. Job creation, especially for less skilled and unemployed individuals.

xii. Market viability, often cheaper than fired bricks, dependent on local context.

xiii. Reduction in imports, owing to local production and unskilled labor utilization.

xiv. Flexible production scales, spanning from manual to motorized tools.

xv. Cost-effectiveness, stemming from local production and minimal transport.

Earth remains a primary building method in many developing countries, being easily accessible, cost-effective, and suitable for unskilled individuals. Its high thermal insulation, fire resistance, and thermal comfort contribute to its appeal. Earth-based construction methods, such as adobe blocks and wattle and daub, have been used for centuries. Moreover, compressed earth, a blend of soil and stabilizers compacted under high pressure, enhances performance and strength, despite the inherent heavy and weak properties of soil.

Durability challenges persist in earthen houses, prompting suggestions from past researchers for enhancing the strength and durability of earth raw materials. Strategies include using stabilizers, appropriate architectural design, reinforcing with bonding mortar, and applying protective plaster or render. While rendering, paint, or plaster can shield a compressed earth block or housing wall from external threats, their cost and disparities in expansion rates between these materials and soil blocks pose limitations.

4. Methodology (laboratory preparation and results)

Palm kernel shells were dried in sunlight and burnt following BS specifications. Two types of blocks, Control Mix Block (CMB) and Cement-PKSA Block (CPB), were produced using lateritic soil. The variables included cement-PKSA ratio, compaction pressure, and curing conditions. CMB was stabilized with 10% cement, while CPB was prepared with mix ratios of 8:2, 6:4, 4:6, and 2:8 (Cement: PKSA). Compaction pressures of 6 and 10 MPa were applied to create 66 CMB and 528 CPB of dimensions 100 x 100 x 100 mm. The blocks underwent curing at 100% humidity followed by 28 days of secondary curing. Wet and Dry Compressive Strength tests (WCS and DCS) were conducted according to BS standards. The influence of mix hold-back times (5, 30, 60, 90, and 120 minutes) on compressive strength was examined. Block Dry Density (BDD) and Total Water Absorption (TWA) were also determined as per BS specifications. The data were statistically analyzed using ANOVA at $\alpha 0.05$.

For CMB at 6 MPa, WCS was 8.99 MPa, while CPB values were 9.84, 7.51, 5.29, and 3.21 MPa for mix ratios of 8:2, 6:4, 4:6, and 2:8, respectively. At 10 MPa, CPB exhibited values of 10.11, 8.41, 6.72, and 5.76 MPa, respectively. DCS values at 6 MPa for mix ratios of 8:2, 6:4, 4:6, and 2:8 were 11.79, 9.66, 7.33, and 4.61 MPa, respectively. These surpassed the recommended standards of 3.00 and 4.12 MPa for WCS and DCS, respectively. An inverse relationship was noted between WCS and hold-back time; WCS values were 5.28, 5.13, 4.41, 2.59, and 2.07 MPa for hold-back times of 5, 30, 60, 90, and 120 minutes, respectively. BDD for CMB and CPB at 6 MPa was

2128 ± 0.33 kg/m^3 and 2132 ± 0.095 kg/m^3, respectively, and 2127 ± 0.01 kg/m^3 at 10 MPa, meeting the required 2000 kg/m^3 standard. TWA was 7.5% for CMB and 7.0% for CPB, both within the 12% standard. A 44% TWA decrease and 2.3% density increase were achieved with variations in cement content from 2 to 8%. The correlation coefficient and P-values were significant, indicating a positive relationship between BDD and WCS, and a negative relationship between TWA and BDD for both CMB and CPB.

Thus, palm kernel shell ash proves suitable as a partial cement replacement for producing compressed stabilized earth blocks.

5. Waste to wealth opportunity

Throughout history, waste derived from agricultural and industrial activities has led to challenges related to waste management and environmental contamination. Nonetheless, the construction industry has the potential to harness the practical and cost-effective advantages offered by these agricultural and industrial waste materials [2]. These waste materials, often available locally and lacking commercial value, result in minimized transportation expenses [3]. Particularly in the realm of economical construction, agricultural waste materials can offer advantages over conventional alternatives. By incorporating waste materials into construction processes, the conservation of natural resources and environmental safeguards are promoted. Despite the considerable difficulties associated with the disposal and handling of industrial and agricultural waste, their utilization not only safeguards resources but also contributes to environmental preservation and reduces construction expenditures. This approach becomes viable due to the availability of waste materials at negligible or no cost, resulting in substantial contributions to the conservation of natural resources and the ecological equilibrium.

Given the substantial presence and volume of waste products worldwide, environmental risks and disposal challenges have come to the forefront. Nigeria's "Waste to Wealth policy" provides a framework for treating waste materials and subsequently utilizing them to enhance or stabilize soils with suboptimal geotechnical properties, particularly expansive soils. Many of these materials are sourced locally from traditional industrial and agricultural waste, including Palm Kernel Shell Ash (PKSA), maize cobs, Saw Dust Ash (SDA), coconut shell ash, rice husk, Locust beans ash, and Cocoa Pod ash. Typically, these materials originate from milling facilities, thermal power plants, and waste management installations [4–6].

Scientific exploration has delved into the feasibility of integrating agricultural waste materials into both building construction and civil engineering projects. Additionally, within the realm of oil palm manufacturing, specific waste products warrant consideration. One such by-product is Palm Oil Fuel Ash (POFA), which emerges from palm fruit residues derived from oil palm trees. The oil palm industry utilizes fresh fruit bunches as its primary raw material, yet the processing of these bunches generates substantial waste, including empty fruit bunches, shells, and fibers. Following the extraction of oil from the palm fruit bunches, roughly 70% of raw waste is produced. This waste can be classified into three categories: fruit-kernel shells, fiber husks, and gels. Notably, kernel shells and fiber husks are burned as fuel in oil palm mills, generating energy within the temperature range of 450 to 600 degrees Celsius. Subsequent to combustion, approximately 15% of solid waste materializes as oil palm fuel ash and palm kernel shell ash. The ash's color varies from light to dark gray shades, contingent on its carbon content, with uniformity achieved through pulverization. Notably, there have been endeavors to substitute fine aggregate with palm kernel shell ash, often employing palm oil fuel ash as an admixture due to the pozzolanic properties of palm kernel shell ash when combined with cement.

6. Conclusion

In the pursuit of advancing sustainable construction practices, the exploration of unconventional materials and innovative techniques emerges as a pivotal avenue for shaping the trajectory of the built environment. This chapter has undertaken a meticulous examination of the feasibility and potential merits associated with utilizing waste sourced from *Elaeis guineensis*, or the African oil palm, as a partial cement substitute within the context of compressed earth block stabilization. Through an intricate dissection of the benefits, challenges, and practical implications inherent in this approach, it becomes discernible that this novel methodology holds substantial promise for significantly influencing sustainable construction practices.

The amalgamation of *Elaeis guineensis* waste into the stabilization process of compressed earth blocks embodies a dual-purpose solution: It effectively addresses the imperative matter of waste management in the palm oil production industry while concurrently augmenting the mechanical and thermal attributes of the resultant construction blocks. This symbiotic synergy encapsulates the core ethos of sustainability by mitigating environmental impact while concurrently enhancing structural integrity. The comprehensive examination spanning scientific, engineering, and pragmatic domains demonstrates a compelling pathway toward a more ecologically conscious and resource-efficient paradigm in the construction domain.

Concluding this discourse, it emerges that the utilization of *Elaeis guineensis* waste as a partial cement replacement within compressed earth block stabilization represents not a singular panacea but rather a fragment within a broader panorama. It epitomizes the convergence of diverse disciplines encompassing agricultural practices, waste management protocols, material science intricacies, and construction engineering methodologies, all coalescing toward the common aspiration of sustainable progress. The success intrinsic to this innovative approach resides not solely in the confines of laboratory innovation but equally in the successful transposition of these innovations to real-world contexts, where their true potential is effectively harnessed.

Ultimately, the integration of waste materials from *Elaeis guineensis* into the process of stabilizing compressed earth blocks highlights the effectiveness of working across different fields, innovative thinking, and careful planning. By adopting this new method and understanding its core ideas, the construction industry is ready for a significant change. This change represents a shift where environmental challenges are reduced, the ability to withstand challenges is strengthened, and the overall structure of the built environment aligns with the principles of sustainability. This transformation benefits both the current generation and those to come.

Author details

Adeola Sarah Ajayi
Department of Architecture, University of Ibadan, Nigeria

*Address all correspondence to: ayangadeanthonia@gmail.com

References

[1] Riza FV, Rahman IA, Ahmad Zaidi AM. A brief review of compressed stabilised earth blocks. In: International Conference on Science and Social Research (CSSR). Malaysia: Kuala Lumpur; 2010. pp. 999-1004

[2] Chandra S, Berntsson L. Lightweight Aggregate Concrete Science Technology Application. New York: Noyes Publication; 2002. pp. 231-240

[3] Abdul-Rahman H. Some observations on the issue of quality cost in construction. International Journal of Quality & Reliability Management. 1997;**14**(5):464-481

[4] Bheel N, Mangi S, Lal S. Coconut Shell ash as cementitious material in concrete: A review. Jurnal Kejuruteraan. 2021;**33**:27-38

[5] Ikeagwuani CC, Obeta IN, Agunwamba JC. Stabilization of black cotton soil subgrade using sawdust ash and lime. Soils and Foundations. 2019;**59**(1):162-175

[6] Zaid O, Ahmad J, Siddique MS, Aslam F. Effect of incorporation of Rice husk ash instead of cement on the performance of steel fibers reinforced concrete. Frontiers in Materials. 2021;**8**:66562, 1-66514

Chapter 4

Congo: The Next Frontier for the Palm Oil Industry

Mpoko Bokanga

Abstract

The oil palm (*Elaeis guineensis* Jacq.) originated in West and Central Africa. Some of the earliest scientific breakthroughs that led to the development of the palm oil industry were made in the Democratic Republic of Congo (DRC, earlier known as the Belgian Congo); these include the elucidation of the genetics of the kernel shell thickness and the identification of the basic engineering principles for palm oil extraction. In the past 50 years, Indonesia and Malaysia rapidly expanded palm oil production to account today for over 80% of the world palm oil supply. This accelerated development has significantly contributed to the socioeconomic development of those two countries, but has raised concerns regarding environmental sustainability. Current level of knowledge makes it possible to mitigate the negative impact of palm oil on the environment and to achieve Net-Zero Emission targets. The palm oil industry has proven its ability to lift millions of people out of poverty. With plentiful suitable land, diverse oil palm genetic resources, abundant labor, large palm oil local and regional markets, and commitment to sustainable palm oil sector, the DRC should become the next frontier for palm oil and chart the course for responsible development of a palm oil industry that contributes to human prosperity, social progress, and environmental protection.

Keywords: *Elaeis guineensis*, palm oil, sustainability, net-zero emissions, Democratic Republic of Congo

1. Introduction

The oil palm (*Elaeis guineensis* Jacq.) originated in the rain forest of West and Central Africa but is now commercially grown throughout the tropical belt, with a high concentration in Southeast Asia. It arrived in South America in the 16th century but did not reach Asia until the middle of the 19th century [1]. It is in Southeast Asia that, in the second half of the 20th century, the growing of oil palm on a commercial scale for oil production developed rapidly; Indonesia and Malaysia today produce 87% of the global output of palm oil. In just fifty years, between 1970 and 2020, the world combined production of oil from the oil palm increased over 37-fold, from 2.31 million metric tons in 1970 to 87.32 million metric tons in 2020. The market share of palm oil relative to the other vegetable oils grew from 17% in 1970 to 42% in 2020 [2].

Palm oil is today found in nearly 60% of all packaged products in supermarkets because of its versatility and low cost relative to the other vegetable oils. In its refined form, palm oil is used as an ingredient in a wide range of foods, such as margarine, confectionery, chocolate, ice cream and bakery products where it contributes taste and texture [3]. Palm oil is also used in a variety of non-food applications including soaps and detergents, cosmetics, pharmaceuticals, and biofuels. Due to its versatility, and because the oil palm produces about ten times more oil per hectare of land than any other oilseed crop, demand for palm oil will continue to rise in the foreseeable future. The global palm oil market size, which was valued at USD 62.94 billion in 2021, is projected to reach USD 99.41 billion by 2030, a compounded annual growth rate (CAGR) of 5.21% for the period [4]. According to Afriyanti et al. [5], the world demand for cooking oil and biodiesel by 2050 could rise to between 264–447 million metric tons of which Indonesia could provide 39–60%. Other palm oil producing countries are expected to fill the remaining gap.

The rapid expansion of the palm oil industry, particularly in Malaysia and Indonesia, has generated mixed results; while it has been associated with perceived negative social and environmental impacts, it has led to positive benefits, including large fiscal revenues for producing countries and significant regular income streams that have taken out of poverty millions of smallholder growers involved in oil palm cultivation [6, 7].

In the past ten years, countries in South America have been rapidly expanding their acreage under oil palm while avoiding deforestation and guided by roundtable certification programs [8, 9]. With the current body of knowledge, plans are being developed to enable continued expansion of oil palm cultivation up to the year 2050 in Indonesia and Malaysia without deforestation and on peat-free land [4, 10, 11].

This chapter submits that the next frontier for the growth of the palm oil industry is in Africa, and particularly in the Democratic Republic of Congo (DRC) where abundance of land, unique and diverse oil palm genetic resources, suitable weather, cheap labor, access to a large consumer base make it possible for this country to become a significant contributor to meeting the growing demand for palm oil. This can be achieved while contributing to the global effort of achieving the Net-Zero Emissions target [12–14]. The chapter gives a brief history of palm oil production and trade, describes the early discoveries made in Congo that led to the establishment of the palm oil industry in the world, and discusses lessons learned from the expansion of palm oil in Asia and Latin America that could be utilized to chart the course of a new development of the palm oil industry in a way that contributes to human prosperity, social progress and environmental protection.

2. Brief history of palm oil

The rain forest of West and Central Africa is the center of origin of the oil palm (*Elaeis guineensis*). Its fruits were taken to other parts of the world between the 14th and 19th centuries. Palm oil (PO), extracted from the mesocarp of the oil palm fruit, and palm kernel oil (PKO) that is expressed from the fruit endocarp inside the kernel have been used for food, cosmetic and therapeutic applications in Africa for thousands of years. Wild and semi-wild groves of oil palm are found in the humid belt of Africa, from the coastal areas of West Africa to the Congo basin in Central Africa [1].

There is archaeological evidence that palm oil was taken to as far as Egypt since a mass of several kilograms of it was found in the excavation of an early tomb dated to 3000 B.C. [15]. It is at the beginning of the 20th century that commercial scale planting of oil palm started mainly to supply the production of soap and margarine in Europe [16]. In 1911, Sir William Leverhulme, founder of the Lever Brothers company, arrived in Congo with an authorization from the Belgian Minister of Colonies to develop the palm oil business with access to a concession of about 750,000 ha [17]. The company he founded, *Huileries du Congo Belge (HCB)*, is still in operation in the palm oil business today, although under a different name, *Plantations et Huileries du Congo (PHC)*. Such a large concession was given to Leverhulme with a mandate to study the rational utilization of wild palm groves and find the technical basis for establishing plantations; to study the extraction methods for palm oil and the handling of palm kernels; to study appropriate transport and storage methods for palm products and to identify markets and industrial outlets for palm products [18]. In 1910, Congo exported 2160 tons of palm oil and 6140 tons of palm kernels. By 1957, the volume of export of palm oil had grown to 150,000 tons [19].

In Indonesia, the first commercial scale planting of oil palm is said to have been introduced by Adrien Hallet [20], a Belgian national who acquired the knowledge of planting oil palm in Congo [18, 21]. In 1911, Hallet established a plantation in Sumatra using seedlings obtained from the Buitenzorg (now Bogor) Botanical Garden. In Malaysia, Henri Fauconnier is credited with starting the first true oil palm plantation in 1917 at Tennamaran Estate in Batang Berjuntai, Selangor [22]. In the 1960s, the Malaysian government promoted the cultivation of oil palm through the agricultural diversification programme to reduce the country's dependence on rubber and tin, and to alleviate rural poverty [23]. The palm oil industry in Malaysia is credited with consistently contributing toward poverty eradication and narrowing the income gap between rural and urban residents [24, 25]. Palm oil has been shown to contribute to the sustainable development goals (SDG) more than any other vegetable oil [26].

In 2022/2023, global production of palm oil was estimated at 76 million metric tons, a 4% increase over the 73 million produced in 2020/2021 [27]. Although world trade of palm oil started with production from Africa in the late 19th century, today Indonesia and Malaysia account for over 83% of the total production while the African production has been reduced to a mere 4% [28].

3. Early days of the palm oil trade

In Africa, wild or semi-wild groves of oil palm have been used for thousands of years to produce oil for food, cosmetic and therapeutic uses [16]. There is archeological evidence that palm oil was traded as early as 3000 years ago, as several kilograms of it were found inside an ancient tomb in Egypt [1, 15]. Palm oil is reported to have been exported from West Africa to England as early as in 1790 [1]. But it is in the 1850s that the trade of palm oil between Africa and Europe developed, mainly to support the production of soap in England [29]. By 1870, up to 30,000 metric tons of palm oil extracted from the fruits of oil palms growing in wild and semi-wild groves were being exported to England from British colonies in West Africa. Palm kernels were also being exported in even larger quantities [30] for use in soap manufacturing and candle making. Palm kernel oil was preferred in those applications because the lather produced from it was more satisfying, and the candles were odorless upon burning. Palm oil was also perfectly suited to use as an industrial lubricant, for oiling engine parts and in tinplate production [29].

In Congo, export of palm oil and palm kernel started in the 19th century. In 1910, it was recorded that 2160 tons of palm oil and 6140 tons of palm kernel were exported to Europe, mainly England for the oil and Germany for the kernel [19, 31]. By 1960, the export of palm oil had risen to 167,000 tons, making palm oil export from Congo second only to Nigeria and ahead of Malaysia and Indonesia [18, 19]. While Congo produced 224,000 tons of palm oil in 1961, Malaysia and Indonesia produced 94,846 tons and 145,700 tons respectively. Sixty years later, Congo's production was stagnating at 300,000 tons, while Malaysia's and Indonesia's production had exponentially grown to 19.1 million tons and 44.8 million tons respectively. The next section shows that the technological bases of the palm oil industry were laid in Congo. However, those innovations did not benefit Congo or African producing countries. Instead, cooperation and competition between two different clusters in former colonial territories in Africa and Asia enabled the rise of palm oil as a global commodity in Indonesia and Malaysia [29].

4. Technological foundations of the oil palm industry

4.1 Genetic control of the *Tenera* phenotype

Some of the earliest scientific breakthroughs that led to the development of the palm oil industry were made in the Democratic Republic of Congo (earlier known as the Belgian Congo). These include the elucidation of the genetic basis of an important trait in *Elaeis guineensis*: kernel shell thickness. Fruits of the oil palm have kernels that may have a thick shell, a thin shell or no shell at all. Oil palm geneticists have called the palms with large kernel and thick shell the *Dura* form, the ones with small kernel and thin shell are called the *Tenera* form and, the palms without kernel shell are the *Pisifera* form [1]. Fruits of palms of the *Tenera* form contain more oil than those of the *Dura* form since in the *Tenera* form, the mesocarp represents 55–96% of the fruit, while the mesocarp in the Dura form only represents 35–65% of the fruit.

Genetic studies undertaken in the 1930s at the INEAC (*Institut d'Etudes Agronomiques du Congo*) research station located at Yagambi, DRC by Beirnaert and Vanderweyen [32] revealed that the kernel shell thickness was controlled by a single gene with two codominant alleles. The genome of palms of the *Dura* form carries two *sh+* alleles, while palms of the *Pisifera* type carries two *sh-* alleles. The *Tenera* form was identified as a hybrid between the Dura and Pisifera forms as it carries one *sh+* allele and one *sh-* allele. As early as 1946, Vanderweyen was able to demonstrate that by crossing *Dura* and *Pisifera* forms (called DxP cross), one could obtain 100% *Tenera* progenies [33, 34]. Crosses between two *Tenera* gave progenies that segregated according to Mendel's heredity law into 25% *Dura* form, 25% *Pisifera* form and 50% *Tenera* form. This was called the "Congo theory" and it was later confirmed in Nigeria [35] and in Malaysia [36]. The DxP cross has become the norm today for producing *Tenera* seedlings for planting in all commercial oil palm plantations and constitute an important basis for the genetic improvement of oil palm productivity [37].

4.2 Engineering principles of palm oil extraction

Another scientific achievement that greatly contributed to the growth of the palm oil industry and trade was the establishment of the basic engineering principles of the palm oil extraction process that were published in 1955 in the Mongana Report [38]. The Association of producers and exporters of oil palm of Belgian Congo, known under their French acronym CONGOPALM, set up a pilot plant at Mongana in DRC to investigate in detail the scientific, engineering and technoeconomic principles of processing oil palm fresh fruit bunches (FFB) into industrial grade palm oil. Their investigations were conducted between 1952 and 1955. Their findings were published in what is known today by all palm oil mill engineers as the "Mongana Report" [38, 39]. Over sixty years after it was published, the Mongana report continues to guide the design and operation of palm oil mills around the world [40].

5. Growth of the palm oil industry

In the second half of the 20th century, the development of the palm oil industry received a very strong impetus, mainly from Malaysia and Indonesia. Between 1960 and 2010, global palm oil production has almost doubled every ten years, thanks to the output from these two countries [41]. Such an achievement does not come about by chance. In 1956, the Malaysian government established the Federal Land Development Authority (FELDA) with the objective of poverty eradication through the cultivation of oil palm and rubber [42, 43]. The authority oversaw land development and allocation to settlers, facilitating access to finance by planters, as well as implementing downstream projects covering the entire crop value chain and generating its own income through a variety of businesses and corporate entities such as the FELDA Holding Berhad, Felda Plantation Sdn Bhd and Felda Global Ventures (FGV).

In Indonesia, between 1967 and 1997, palm oil production increased 20-fold [44]. Although support to plantation agriculture was included in Indonesia's development plans since the 1950s, it is only in the late 1970s that sustained efforts were applied with the Nucleus Estate Scheme (NES) (*Perkebunan Inti Rakyat*; PIR), whereby state-owned plantation companies (the 'nucleus') helped smallholder farmers (namely plasma farmers) to grow oil palm [45]. Support to the palm oil industry came in three phases. First there was direct involvement of the government with state-owned companies having access to land and to institutional support. The scheme was implemented at the same time as a transmigration program. The state-owned nucleus estate held 20% of the land, while the relocated smallholders were allocated 80% of the land and received technical assistance from the nucleus estate. This so-called PIR-trans phase lasted from 1986 to 1994. In the second phase called KKPA (*Koperasi Kredit Primer untuk Anggota*; Primary Cooperative Credit for Members) between 1995 and 1998, the door was opened to foreign direct investment in large scale plantations but following the private-community partnership model tested in the PIR-Trans phase. After 1998, the Indonesian government shifted to a liberalization policy based on decentralization and encouraging public–private partnerships between market actors and the government, and social–private partnerships between market actors and smallholder communities but following a market-driven model [45]. Between 1970 and 2000, Malaysia and Indonesia have experienced economic growth and structural changes that have brought with them rural poverty reduction and improved living standards, all linked to, among other things, the growth of the palm oil industry [46, 47].

While the palm oil industry was growing and contributing to social and economic development of Malaysia and Indonesia, technical collaboration on oil palm plantation technology was on-going between palm oil producing countries of Southeast Asia and Africa [29, 48]. Several private companies were involved in the oil palm business in both clusters of producing countries. The main difference was government policies and support. In Congo, for instance, the government of the then Republic of Zaire nationalized all foreign owned businesses, including farms and plantations [49]. Nationalized businesses were handed over to local citizens to manage. Many of them, including oil palm plantations collapsed and never recovered. Fifty years later, the missed opportunities have become evident to policy makers and to potential investors. In April 2023, the government of the DRC established the *Conseil consultatif présidentiel pour le pacte national de l'agriculture et de l'alimentation* (CCP-PNAA; Presidential Consulative Counci for the Food and Agriculture National Compact) which will be tasked with, among other things, designing and recommending policies to facilitate private investments in agriculture [50].

6. Opportunities for the DR Congo

6.1 Increasing demand for vegetable oils

The global vegetable oil market is expected to grow in value at over 7% per year from USD 318 billion in 2022 to reach USD 791 billion by 2031, with the palm oil segment being the biggest contributor to this growth [4]. Demand for vegetable oils over the past two decades has been driven by a combination of population growth, changing dietary patterns, economic development, and evolving consumer preferences. The specific trends and types of vegetable oils in demand may vary by region and market, but overall, this increase in demand has made vegetable oils a crucial component of modern diets and industries, and is expected to continue.

Palm oil has evolved to become one of the most widely consumed and traded vegetable oils globally, with its demand driven by its cost efficiency, versatility, and suitability for a wide range of products and applications. It is estimated that more than half of all packaged products consumed in the USA, including lipstick, soaps, detergents and even ice cream, contain palm oil [51]. The market share of palm oil compared to the other vegetable oils has steadily grown from 13.6% in 1961 to 36.5% in 2020 [2]. Palm oil is now the most traded vegetable oil in the world. The very high productivity of oil palm in terms of quantity of oil produced per hectare of land, which is five to ten times the productivity of other oilseed crops, gives palm oil a major role in meeting the demand for vegetable oil while maintaining a low ecological footprint. Environmental concerns have been raised regarding the rapid expansion of oil palm cultivation in Malaysia and Indonesia [52, 53]. While these countries are taking steps to address those issues, other palm oil producing countries, such as DRC, have a clear opportunity to contribute to meeting this growing demand.

6.2 Abundant and suitable land, favorable weather

With 2.345 million square kilometers, the DRC is the second largest country in Africa after Algeria. Development agencies estimate that the country has over 80 million hectares of arable land, of which less than 10% is currently under cultivation [54, 55]. This figure concerns general agriculture and has always been used by the Ministry of Agriculture. In 2019, a team of researchers assessed the available land suitable for growing oil palm in the Congo Basin, of which 60% is contained in the DRC. Their data suggest that up to 280 million hectares could be suitable for oil palm cultivation in the Congo Basin, including 167 million hectares in the DRC alone [56]. The model used to calculate this land does not include primary forest. In fact, of the total suitable area available in DRC, only 13% is found in protected areas, meaning that 145 million hectares are found in areas that are compatible with current environmental standards such as the Roundtable on Sustainable Palm Oil (RSPO) [57].

It should be noted here that DRC and other African countries of West and Central Africa signed the Marrakech Declaration in November 2016 during COP-22 committing themselves to sustainable development of the palm oil value chain with the support of the private sector and civil society organizations in what is known as the African Palm Oil Initiative [58]. These countries support the development of oil palm plantations but with a commitment to zero-deforestation. The Ministry of Agriculture in the DRC has targeted over 2000 farms and plantations abandoned since the 1973 nationalization for immediate development [59]; many of these plantations used to be under oil palm cultivation and could be rapidly brought back into production.

The climate of the DRC, with mean surface air temperature of 24–28°C and over 1500 mm of rainfall, is well suited to the oil palm cultivation. Straddling the Equator, the rainfall distribution throughout the year is rather uniform with a short dry period that grows longer as one get farther away from the Equator line.

While oil palm development can affect climate change, mainly by increasing carbon emission through deforestation and biodiversity loss, it is also true that climate change will affect the capacity of lands to produce palm oil [60]. It is therefore imperative to think of how the suitability for oil palm cultivation will be affected by climate change. Paterson et al [61] have described the CLIMEX mechanistic niche model which can be used to estimate the evolution of the scenarios of suitable growing areas for oil palm under climate change in Africa. With this CLIMEX tool, Paterson has shown that the highly suitable and suitable areas for growing palm oil between now and 2050 were concentrated in the DRC, with these areas expected to become less suitable after 2050 [62]. However, DRC will remain the region with the highest availability of suitable land for oil palm production.

6.3 Availability of adapted genetic resources

The name "Yangambi" is found in the pedigree of elite oil palm varieties planted in many countries with a well-established palm oil industry [48, 63]. While the origin of the parent material has not been clearly determined, the Yangambi trait is usually associated with high yield [48, 63]. Yangambi is a town in the DRC that was the home of *Institut national pour l'étude agronomique du* Congo *belge (*INEAC) where, in the 1930s-1940s, the relationship between the *Dura*, *Pisifera* and *Tenera* forms of the oil palm was elucidated [1, 32, 33]. Its coordinates are 0.767475°N and 24.441404°E (https://en.wikipedia.org/wiki/Yangambi). The use of this name for the oil palm material suggest that this material originated from the research station. Since DRC occupies a large proportion of the Congo Basin which is part of the center of diversity of the oil palm, it should be expected that material similar to, or even with better performance characteristics than, the Yangambi line that was taken to southeast Asia could be found. The oil palm is found naturally growing in a diversity of microclimates in DRC. An extensive prospection of local land races will certainly uncover new lines with genetic attributes that might prove useful to produce new varieties that will withstand the effects of climate changes.

6.4 Availability of labor and the poverty reduction imperative

The DRC population stands today at 102 million people [64] with 54% living in the rural areas. The unemployment rate is officially set at 4.99% for 2022 [65], but this figure represents the share of the labor force that is without work but available for and seeking employment. In the rural areas where opportunities for employment are scarce, people engage in subsistence agriculture, in petty trading or are self-employed without being registered with an employment service and therefore are not counted as unemployed. The number of people in need of a regular income is very high. The minimum wage in DRC is set by law at 7,075 Congolese Francs (EUR 3) per worker per day [66]. In 2022, it was estimated at USD 92.47 per month [67], significantly lower than in Malaysia, where the minimum wage was raised from RM1,200 to RM1,500 (about USD 320) per month from 1 July 2023 [68], and lower than in Indonesia, where minimum wages range from USD 126 to USD 316 depending on the location [69].

6.5 Access to a large palm oil consumer base

The production of palm oil in DRC is primarily targeted at satisfying the local demand for this commodity. In 2022, palm oil consumption in DRC was estimated at 425,000 metric tons [70], while domestic production is currently estimated at 300,000 metric tons [71]. Palm oil is consumed daily by the over 100 million people of DRC. Local prices for the commodity vary widely between location, from CDF 3,000 to CDF 6,000 per liter, equivalent to USD 1.25 to USD 2.50 per liter [72].

A strong demand for palm oil exists in all the countries around the DRC. In 2019, the demand for palm oil of African countries was 7.31 million metric tons. Against a local production of only 2.79 million tons [73]. This demand grew at over 6% per year for the period 2010–2019 and is expected to continue to grow at this rate in the coming years. As a member of three trading and customs unions in Africa (Economic Community of Central African States (ECCAS), East African Community (EAC), and Southern Africa Development Conference (SADC)) and having joined the treaty of the African Continental Free Trade Agreement on January first 2021 [74], DRC is uniquely positioned to export to all the countries of the continent estimated to contain over one billion consumers.

6.6 Lessons learned from Malaysia and Indonesia

The accelerated development of the palm oil industry in southeast Asia has led to many concerns being raised regarding environmental sustainability of the palm oil industry. It has been estimated that 17% of the new plantations in Malaysia and 63% of those in Indonesia came at the direct expense of biodiversity-rich tropical forests over the period 1990–2010 [75–78], and up to 30% of this expansion occurred on peat soils, leading to large CO_2 emissions [79–81]. On the other hand, in Indonesia and Malaysia, which together account for around 85% of global palm oil production, the palm oil industry is credited for lifting millions of people out of poverty by creating millions of well-paying jobs in rural areas where alternative employment opportunities are scarce and enabling tens of thousands of smallholder farmers to own their own land [82]. In its State of Sustainability Initiatives report, the International Institute for Sustainable Development has estimated that in Indonesia and Malaysia, the palm oil sector employs almost 5 million smallholders and workers and a further 6 million people indirectly, while being responsible for nearly 3 million downstream jobs in importing countries [83].

To become the next frontier for the palm oil industry, DRC will need to focus on generating the positive impact that the palm oil industry has produced in southeast

Asia while avoiding or minimizing the negative consequences, especially on climate change and biodiversity. The state of knowledge today makes both objectives achievable. Some of the actions that could be undertaken are briefly mentioned below:

6.6.1 Identify socio-economic impact targets for the palm oil industry

The socio-economic impact of palm oil is complex and varies depending on several factors, including the region, local communities, and the practices of palm oil producers. Key aspects include employment in locations where few opportunities exist; income generation opportunities for rural dwellers with very few alternatives enabling them to support their families and improve their living standards; rural development opportunities through improved infrastructure such as roads and access to markets, which can stimulate economic growth and development in these regions; increased government revenues through tax payments; increased export earnings when palm oil is exported; technology and knowledge transfer on palm oil production and agriculture in general which can benefit local farmers and communities by improving agricultural practices; facilitated market access for other agricultural products and commodities, boosting the income of smallholder farmers and diversifying local economies.

However, there are negative socio-economic challenges that need to be considered and monitored and whose impact needs to be minimized. These include land displacement, particularly of indigenous communities and smallholder farmers; social disputes and conflicts over land ownership leading to social tension and unrest that can arise in areas where palm oil plantations are expanded; poor working conditions including low wages, and inadequate labor rights that can lead to social inequality and exploitation; workers' health concerns due to the use of pesticides and other chemicals in palm oil cultivation, affecting both workers and nearby communities; community health and well-being such as air and water pollution that can have direct health and well-being implications for local communities.

The socio-economic impact of palm oil is multifaceted. While it can provide employment, income, and development opportunities, it is also associated with challenges related to land displacement, social conflicts, working conditions, and environmental impact. The overall impact depends on various factors, including the practices of palm oil producers, government regulations, and efforts to promote sustainable and responsible palm oil production. Efforts to mitigate the negative socio-economic consequences of palm oil production often involve promoting sustainable and responsible practices, ensuring land tenure rights, and supporting smallholder farmers and local communities in palm oil-producing regions.

DRC has a young and rapidly growing population that needs access to adequate infrastructure and income opportunities. The example of Indonesia and Malaysia shows that such opportunities can be provided by the palm oil industry. In DRC, *Plantation et Huileries du Congo*, which with 30,000 ha of planted oi palm and three palm oil mills, is the largest private sector employer in the country, and through the social services it offers to its workers and neighboring communities, is the largest private provider of health services. It builds schools, maintains roads within its area of operations and supports local communities with development programs, facilitates the acquisition and distribution of primary and fast-moving consumer goods in the remote rural locations where it operates. This company intends to generate biogas from its palm oil mill effluents and converts that biogas to electricity, some of which will be made available to local communities that are currently disconnected from the national electricity grid.

The social and economic benefits that can accrue from the palm oil industry need to be quantified and set as national goals against which the growth of the industry in DRC would be measured.

6.6.2 Address environmental impact issues

Key environmental concerns associated with palm oil include deforestation, because the oil palm is naturally suited for growth in the forest ecology. Large areas of rainforests and other natural ecosystems, particularly in Southeast Asia (Indonesia and Malaysia), have been cleared to make way for oil palm plantations. Deforestation can lead to the loss of biodiversity, disruption of ecosystems, and the release of stored carbon dioxide into the atmosphere. The clearing of large tracks of land for palm oil plantations destroys the habitats of many endangered and endemic species, potentially putting these species at risk of extinction. The conversion of diverse natural ecosystems into monoculture oil palm plantations leads to a loss of biodiversity as plantations typically support far fewer species than the original forests.

Other negative environmental impact sources include air pollution when land clearing involves burning, and water pollution caused by excessive use of mineral fertilizers and plant protection pesticides on oil palm plantations; the chemicals used for this purpose can contaminate local water sources and negatively affect aquatic ecosystems.

In the past 20 years, substantial efforts have been made to address these environmental concerns. It started with the establishment of the RSPO in 2004 to promote sustainable and responsible palm oil production through adhesion to global standards and multistakeholder governance [57]. The stakeholders involved in this initiative are oil palm producers, palm oil processors or traders, consumer goods manufacturers, retailers, bankers, and investors, environmental or nature conservation NGOs and social or developmental NGOs.

Popkin et al. [84] have shown that increasingly, oil palm plantation and mill managers are adopting management practices that reduce the negative impact of the industry on biodiversity and environmental processes. Such practices include planting high-yielding varieties, optimizing the application of organic and mineral fertilizers and maintaining a very high harvest quality index in fresh fruit bunches sent to the palm oil mill. Other practices include reliance on biological control of pests, the use of biopesticides and leguminous cover crops [85]. Precision agriculture with its information technology-based tools is relied upon to minimize the use of mineral fertilizers, predict the effectiveness of planned best practices, or identify new sites for expansion of oil palm cultivation [86, 87]. The author has visited several oil palm plantations and mills in Indonesia where these and other practices have been adopted and where the objective is not only for their operation to achieve their Net-Zero Emission target, but possibly to become Net Carbon Negative, thus creating a palm oil business that effectively contribute to the global effort of bringing climate change under control and keeping the temperature rise to below 1.5°C required to avoid a climate catastrophe [88].

6.6.3 Adopt enabling policies and enforce regulations

In its quest to become the next frontier of the palm oil industry, DRC will need to formulate and adopt policy and regulations that are required to give rise to a sustainable palm oil industry that addresses all environmental, social, and economic challenges. Some key strategies and initiatives to be considered include the following:

a. Certification programs: Support and promote certification programs, such as the RSPO and adapt the standard to DRC conditions to enable the conformity of DRC smallholder planters to the standard. Key industry actors should be encouraged to join platforms of excellence such as the Palm Oil Innovation Group (https://poig.org/). These programs and associated groups establish and monitor standards for environmentally and socially responsible palm oil production with a focus on conservation, community development, and responsible practices.

b. Commitment to zero-deforestation: Ensure that palm oil producers in DRC adopt a zero-deforestation commitment. This means that palm oil production should not lead to the clearing of primary forests or other high-conservation value areas. Companies operating in the palm oil business should commit to protecting and preserving these areas.

c. Responsible sourcing: Encourage companies throughout the palm oil supply chain, including manufacturers, retailers, and traders, to source palm oil from certified and sustainable sources. This can create market incentives for responsible palm oil production.

d. Support smallholder farmers: Both Indonesia and Malaysia have shown that special programs to support smallholder farmers who cultivate oil palm are important to develop and strengthen the palm oil industry. Smallholder farmers need support with training, technical assistance, and access to resources so that they can in turn adopt more sustainable farming practices.

e. Alternative livelihoods: Not everyone in the rural areas will need to be involved in oil palm. Project for alternative livelihoods for communities should be developed to reduce dependence on palm oil production and help alleviate social and environmental pressures.

f. Conservation and restoration: Mitigate the environmental impact of palm oil production by investing in the conservation and restoration of degraded lands and ecosystems to offset deforestation and habitat destruction.

g. Transparent supply chains: Promote transparency in the palm oil supply chain. Recommend that companies in the palm oil industry disclose their sourcing practices and report on progress toward sustainability goals.

h. Research and innovation: Invest in research and innovation to develop more efficient and environmentally friendly palm oil cultivation methods, such as high-yield, low-impact planting techniques.

i. Government regulations: Governments in palm oil-producing countries should enforce and strengthen regulations related to land use, environmental protection, labor rights, and land tenure to promote responsible palm oil production.

j. Community engagement: Involve local communities in decision-making processes and ensure they benefit from palm oil production. Respect land tenure rights and conduct social impact assessments to assess and mitigate potential negative consequences.

k. Environmental and social impact assessment: Prior to establishing new plantations, conduct thorough assessments of the potential environmental and social impacts of palm oil projects. These assessments should inform project planning and design.

l. Traceability and accountability: Implement systems to trace palm oil throughout the supply chain to ensure that it comes from responsible sources. Hold companies accountable for their sustainability commitments.

Achieving a truly sustainable palm oil industry requires a multi-stakeholder approach involving governments, businesses, non-governmental organizations, local communities, and consumers. The goal should be to balance the economic benefits of palm oil production with environmental and social considerations, ultimately leading to a more responsible and sustainable industry. Efforts to promote sustainability are ongoing, and progress has been made. As it embarks on expanding its palm oil production capability, DRC should formulate policies, regulations and incentives to ensure that the industry will follow a sustainable course and avoid mistakes that were made elsewhere.

6.6.4 Facilitate financing processes

Financial analysis of investment in palm oil shows that it is a very profitable undertaking [89], even though it takes three to four years before income could be generated from a new oil palm plantation. Financial resources required to gainfully participate in the palm oil industry are substantial and often beyond the means of smallholder farmers and low income citizens. Development finance that used to be available from Development Finance Institutions such as the World Bank and the International Finance Corporation stopped in 2009 because of pressure from non-Governmental Organizations but seems to be ready to resume [90].

Public finance for agricultural projects has not been successful in Africa, and in particular in DRC [91, 92]. Innovative approaches are needed that will target progressive private sector companies with clear and verifiable environmental, social and governance (ESG) policies.

7. Conclusion

Countries of the equatorial belt where oil palm can be commercially grown need to use this highly efficient natural source of vegetable oil in the pursuit of their social and economic advancement. At the same time, they have become aware of and are committed to the protection of their natural resources and environment to secure a sustainable future for their generations yet unborn. These two seemingly competing demands can be reconciled, but it will take strong collaboration between producers and users of palm oil to limit, and even reverse, the contribution of the palm oil industry to climate change.

This chapter has shown that the DRC has played a key role in the birth and development of the palm oil industry and that only six decades ago the country was the second largest exporter of palm oil in the world. It has lost that position today and is not even counted among the ten largest palm oil producing countries. Nevertheless, the country's assets needed to become a large producer of palm oil remain intact.

Land, labor, and high-performance oil palm genetic resources are available in large quantity. The weather in DRC is conducive to oil palm cultivation, and even though climate change will most likely reduce the suitability for oil palm production in Africa, science-based projections suggest that the largest area of suitability for oil palm cultivation up to the year 2100 will be in the DRC.

The development of the palm oil industry in the Congo Basin, the largest carbon sink in the world and where historically the palm oil industry began, could be realized in a way that contribute to pathways which limit global warming to 1.5°C as recommended by the Intergovernmental Panel on Climate Change (IPCC) to avoid a climate catastrophe [88]. Innovations that reduce carbon emissions are already in application in oil palm plantation in several countries, while others are in the pipeline. *Plantations et Huileries du Congo*, the largest industrial producer of palm oil in the DRC, has demonstrated that in a very short period of time (less than three years), adoption of science-based, data-driven, environmentally and socially conscious management practices could lead to significant productivity increase enabling the company to meet the triple bottom line of improved welfare for its workers and surrounding communities, sustainability for the planet and acceptable return on investment. This example is offered as a proof of concept upon which a larger program can be built to take DRC back among the key palm oil producing countries.

Conflict of interest

The author is an employee of *Plantations et Huileries du Congo* mentioned in this chapter. However, the statements and ideas expressed in this chapter are solely his own and do not necessarily reflect the position of the company or of its owners. No compensation or favor of any kind has been received for the writing of this chapter.

Author details

Mpoko Bokanga
Plantation et Huileries du Congo, Kinshasa, Democratic Republic of Congo

*Address all correspondence to: mpoko.bokanga@phc-congo.com

References

[1] Corley RHV, Tinker PB. The Oil Palm. Hoboken: Wiley-Blackwell; 2016. DOI: 10.1002/9781118953297

[2] Ourworldindata. 2023. Available from: https://ourworldindata.org/palm-oil [Accessed: October 2023]

[3] Sustainable Palm Oil Choice. 2023. Available from: https://www.sustainablepalmoilchoice.eu/facts-on-palm-oil/ [Accessed: October 2023]

[4] Strait Research. 2023. Available from: https://straitsresearch.com/report/palm-oil-market

[5] Afriyanti D, Kroeze C, Saad A. Indonesia palm oil production without deforestation and peat conversion by 2050. Science of the Total Environment. 2016;**557-558**(2016):562-570. DOI: 10.1016/j.scitotenv.2016.03.032

[6] Kubitza C, Krishna VV, Alamsyah Z, Qaim M. The Economics Behind an Ecological Crisis: Livelihood Effects of Oil Palm Expansion in Sumatra, Indonesia. Springer Science+Business Media, LLC, part of Springer Nature; 2018. DOI: 10.1007/s10745-017-9965-7

[7] Ruml A, Chrisendo D, Iddrisu AM, Alhassan A, Karakara AA, Nuryartono N, et al. Smallholders in agro-industrial production: Lessons for rural development from a comparative analysis of Ghana's and Indonesia's oil palm sectors. Land Use Policy. 2022;**119**:1-14. DOI: 10.1016/j.landusepol.2022.106196

[8] Furumo PR, Mitchell Aide T. Characterizing commercial oil palm expansion in Latin America: land use change and trade. Environment Research Letters. 2017;**12**:024008. DOI: 10.1088/1748-9326/aa5892

[9] Brandão F, Schoneveld G, Pacheco P, Vieira I, Piraux M, Mota D. The challenge of reconciling conservation and development in the tropics: Lessons from Brazil's oil palm governance model. World Development. 2021;**139**:105268

[10] Mosnier A, Boere E, Reumann A, Yowargana P, Pirker J, Havlík P, Pacheco P. Palm oil and likely futures: Assessing the potential impacts of zero deforestation commitments and a moratorium on large-scale oil palm plantations in Indonesia. 2017. DOI: 10.17528/cifor/006468

[11] Austin KG, Mosnier A, Pirker J, McCallum I, Fritz S, Kasibhatla PS. Shifting patterns of oil palm driven deforestation in Indonesia and implications for zero-deforestation commitments. Land Use Policy. 2017;**69**:41-48

[12] Sipayung T. Towards Net Zero Emissions and the Mandatory Palm Gasoline Idea. Vol III, No. 03/03/2022. 2022. Available from: https://palmoilina.asia/jurnal-kelapa-sawit/net-zero-emissions/

[13] Sipayung T. Palm oil industry will become a net carbon sink. Journal of Palm Oil Environment. 2021;**II**(12/47/2021):575-579. Available from: https://palmoilina.asia/jurnal-kelapa-sawit/net-zero-emissions/#9-vol-ii-no-47122021-palm-oil-industry-will-become-a-net-carbon-sink

[14] Lan CC, Phillips J. How Can the Palm Oil Industry Reach Net Zero? 2023. Available from: https://chinadialogue.net/en/climate/how-can-palm-oil-reach-net-zero/

[15] Berger K, Martin S. Palm oil. In: Kiple K, Ornelas K, editors. The

Cambridge World History of Food. Cambridge: Cambridge University Press; 2000. pp. 397-411. DOI: 10.1017/CHOL9780521402149.040

[16] Von Hellermann P. Red gold: A history of palm oil in West Africa. 2021. Available from: https://chinadialogue.net/en/food/red-gold-a-history-of-palm-oil-in-west-africa/

[17] Phillips J. An illustrated history of industrial palm oil. 2021. Available from: https://chinadialogue.net/en/food/illustrated-history-of-industrial-palm-oil/ [Accessed: October 2023]

[18] Ergo AB. Histoire de l'Elaéiculture au Congo Belge. Undated. Available from: https://www.google.com/url?sa=t&rct=j&q=&esrc=s&source=web&cd=&cad=rja&uact=8&ved=2ahUKEwi7m-Dz_82CAxVbnmMGHRezCIEQFnoECBQQAQ&url=https%3A%2F%2Fwww.congoforum.be%2FUpldocs%2Fpalmhisco-5.pdf&usg=AOvVaw3pCeUXHpXAkOwkKD5X10OF&opi=89978449 [Accessed: October 2023]

[19] Nicolaï H. Le Congo et l'huile de palme. Un siècle. Un cycle?, Belgeo [online], 4 | 2013. DOI: 10.4000/belgeo.11772. Available from: http://journals.openedition.org/belgeo/11772 [Accessed: October 2023]

[20] Meijaard E, Sheil D. Oil palm plantations in the context of biodiversity conservation. In: Levin SA, editor. Encyclopedia of Biodiversity. 2nd ed. Vol. 5. Waltham, MA: Academic Press; 2013. pp. 600-612. DOI: 10.1016/B978-0-12-384719-5.00340-3

[21] Leplae E. Le palmier à huile en Afrique, son exploitation au Congo belge et en Extreme-Orient. Brussel, Belgium: Librairie Falk fils; 1939

[22] MPOC. 2023. Available from: www.mpoc.org.my/about-palm-oil/ [Accessed: October 2023]

[23] Courtenay PP. The diversification of Malaysian Agriculture, 1950-80: Objectives and achievements. Journal of Southeast Asian Studies. 1984;**15**(1):166-181. Published By: Cambridge University Press

[24] Ngan SL, Er AC, Yatim P, How BS, Lim CH, Ng WPQ, et al. Social sustainability of palm oil industry: A review. Frontiers in Sustainability. 2022;**3**:855551. DOI: 10.3389/frsus.2022.855551

[25] Ali AT. Malaysia's Move Toward a High-Income Economy: Five Decades of Nation Building—A View from Within. In IMF eLibrary; 2002. pp. 83-92

[26] Obaideen K. Contribution of Vegetable Oils towards Sustainable Development Goals: A Comparative Analysis. Policy Analysis and Development Agency Ministry of Foreign Affairs of The Republic of Indonesia. Jakarta, Indonesia; 2020

[27] Shahbandeh M. Palm oil: Global production volume 2012/13-2022/23. 2023. Available from: https://www.statista.com/statistics/613471/palm-oil-production-volume-worldwide/ [Accessed: November 2023]

[28] Index Mundi. Palm oil production by country in 1000 MT. 2023. Available from: https://www.google.com/url?sa=t&rct=j&q=&esrc=s&source=web&cd=&cad=rja&uact=8&ved=2ahUKEwje9Mvc3OKCAxWZTkEAHYzlB9cQFnoECBkQAQ&url=https%3A%2F%2Fwww.indexmundi.com%2Fagriculture%2F%3Fcommodity%3Dpalm-oil&usg=AOvVaw3nRBnodaU6EY-g7AFn_ulo&opi=89978449

[29] Giacomin V. The transformation of the global palm oil cluster: Dynamics of cluster competition between Africa and Southeast Asia (c.1900-1970). Journal

of Global History. 2018;**13**(3):374-398. DOI: 10.1017/S1740022818000207

[30] Poku K. Small-scale Palm Oil Processing in Africa, FAO Agricultural Services Bulletin 148. Rome, Italy: FAO; 2002

[31] Drachoussoff V, Focan A, Hecq J. Le développement rural en Afrique centrale 1908-1960/1962. In: Synthèses et réflexions, deux volumes. Bruxelles, 1203 p: Fondation Roi Baudouin; 1991

[32] Beirnaert and Vanderweyen. Contribution à l'étude génétique et biométrique des variétés d'Elaeis guineensis Jacquin. INEAC, Bruxelles: Publication de l'INEAC, série scientifique, (n° 27). Bruxelles, Belgique: INEAC; 1941

[33] Vanderweyen. Notions de culture de l'Elaeis au Congo Belge. Bruxelles, Belgique: Publication de la Direction de l'Agriculture ,des Forêts, des Élevages et de la Colonisation; 1952

[34] Vanderweyen R, Moureau J, Buyckx EJE, Geortay G, Chevalier A. Le palmier à huile (Elaeis) et sa culture au Congo. Revue international de Botanique Appliquée et d'Agriculture Tropicale. 1953;**32**(363-364):1-20

[35] Hartley CWS. Oil palm breeding and selection in Nigeria. Journal of the West African Institute of Oil Palm Research. 1957;**2**:108-115

[36] Rosenquist EA. An overview of breeding technology and selection in *Elaeis guineensis*. In: Jalani BS et al., editors. Proceedings of the International Palm Oil Development Conference Agriculture. Kuala Lumpur: Palm Oil Research Institute of Malaysia; 1990. pp. 5-25

[37] Gascon JP, De Berchoux C. Caractéristiques de la production d'*Elaeis guineensis* (Jacq.) de diverses origines et de leurs croisements : application à la sélection du palmier à huile. Oléagineux. 1964;**19**:75-84

[38] Ergo AB. Les Huileries du Congo Belge. Mémoires du Congo Belge et du Ruanda-Urundi. 2011;**19**:6-9. Available from: https://www.google.com/url?sa=t&rct=j&q=&esrc=s&source=web&cd=&cad=rja&uact=8&ved=2ahUKEwjikqWOvM-CAxWyS2wGHerZAsoQFnoECBEQAQ&url=https%3A%2F%2Fwww.memoiresducongo.be%2Fwp-content%2Fuploads%2F2014%2F03%2Fmdc_revue_19.pdf&usg=AOvVaw3LBx5XzghXxfb8wrwQXMB0&opi=89978449

[39] Ravi MN. Evolutionary Changes in Milling Technology – Part 1. Palm Oil Engineering Bulletin No. 61 (Oct–Dec 2001). Mapaysian Palm Oil Board; 2001. pp. 4-11

[40] Ravi MN. Process Review: Part 2. Palm Oil Engineering Bulletin No. 109 (Oct–Dec 2013). pp. 31-35. 2013

[41] United States Department of Agriculture. Oilseeds: World Markets and Trade. 2015. Available from: http://www.fas.usda.gov/data/oilseeds-world-markets-and-trade [Accessed: October 2023]

[42] FELDA. 2023. Available from: https://www.felda.gov.my/en/public/felda/about-felda

[43] Rasiah R, Shahrin A. Development of Palm Oil and Related Products in Malaysia and Indonesia. Paper, University of Malaya. 2006. Available from: economics.dstcentre.com, https://www.academia.edu/50711411/Development_of_Palm_Oil_and_Related_Products_in_Malaysia_and_Indonesia

[44] Machmudin A. Development of Palm Oil Industry in Indonesia. GRIPS

Development Forum. 2022. Available from: https://www.google.com/url?sa=t&rct=j&q=&esrc=s&source=web&cd=&cad=rja&uact=8&ved=2ahUKEwj9i8Hi8M-CAxWsumMGHYFgCh8QFnoECAoQAQ&url=https%3A%2F%2Fwww.grips.ac.jp%2Fteacher%2Foono%2Fhp%2Fcourse%2Fstudent_slides%2F2022%2Fali:palm%2520oil%2520industry.pdf&usg=AOvVaw2WX0FatwAg8YZe3lDcJoAp&opi=89978449

[45] Budidarsono S, Susanti A, Zoomers A. Oil palm plantations in Indonesia: The implications for migration. Settlement/Resettlement and Local Economic Development. 2013. pp. 173-193. DOI: 10.5772/53586

[46] Hill H. What's happened to poverty and inequality in Indonesia over half a century? Asian Development Review. 2021;**38**(1):68-97. DOI: 10.1162/adev_a_00158

[47] Edwards R. Is plantation agriculture good for the poor? Evidence from Indonesia's palm oil expansion. In: Working Paper in Trade and Development, No. 2015/12. Arndt-Corden Department of Economics, Crawford School of Public Policy. Canberra, Australia: ANU College of Asia and the Pacific, Australian National University; 2015

[48] Rajanaidu N, Ainul MM, Kushairi A, Din A. Historical Review of Oil Palm Breeding for the Past 50 Years – Malaysian Journey. 2013. Available from: http://isopb.mpob.gov.my/pdfFile/7th/Paper%201%20HISTORICAL%20REVIEW%20FOR%20OIL%20PALM%20BREEDING%20FOR%20THE%20PAS.pdf

[49] The New York Times. Mobutu seizes alien farming concerns in Zaire. 1973. Available from: https://www.nytimes.com/1973/12/01/archives/mobutu-seizes-alien-farming-concerns-in-zaire.html

[50] Luganywa. RDC: Tshisekedi annonce la création d'une structure qui va concrétiser sa vision de relever le défi de la « revanche du sol sur le sous-sol. 2023. Available from: https://www.google.com/url?sa=t&rct=j&q=&esrc=s&source=web&cd=&cad=rja&uact=8&ved=2ahUKEwix1vOL1NiCAxUjQvEDHUflCqQQFnoECA8QAQ&url=https%3A%2F%2F7sur7.cd%2F2023%2F04%2F16%2Frdc-tshisekedi-annonce-la-creation-dune-structure-qui-va-concretiser-sa-vision-de&usg=AOvVaw39j_4WiWsuY8dFPcgj691X&opi=89978449

[51] World Wildlife Fund. What is Palm Oil? Facts about the Palm Oil Industry. 2023. Available from: https://www.google.com/url?sa=t&rct=j&q=&esrc=s&source=web&cd=&cad=rja&uact=8&ved=2ahUKEwiypqa5zdiCAxWbiFwKHc-7AYEQFnoECAsQAw&url=https%3A%2F%2Fwww.worldwildlife.org%2Findustries%2Fpalm-oil&usg=AOvVaw0bGbkUVD-Ilt3AktBgUmL5&opi=89978449 [Accessed: November 2023]

[52] Dayang Norwana AAB, Kunjappan R, Chin M, Schoneveld G, Potter L, Andriani R. The local impacts of oil palm expansion in Malaysia: An assessment based on a case study in Sabah State. In: Working Paper 78. Bogor, Indonesia: CIFOR; 2011

[53] Obidzinski K, Andriani R, Komarudin H, Andrianto A. Environmental and social impacts of oil palm plantations and their implications for biofuel production in Indonesia. Ecology and Society. 2012;**17**(1):25. DOI: 10.5751/ES-04775-170125

[54] IFAD. Democratic Republic of the Congo Country strategic opportunities programme (2019-2024). 2023. Available from: https://www.ifad.org/en/web/

operations/w/country/democratic-republic-of-the-congo [Accessed: November 2023]

[55] Journal CD. La RDC dispose de 80 millions d'hectares de terres arables. 2016. Available from: http://journal.cd/la-rdc-dispose-de-80-millions-dhectares-de-terres-arables-affirme-matata-ponyo-dans-son-livre-pour-un-congo-emergent/

[56] Ordway EM, Sonwa DJ, Levang M, Boringong F, Miaro L, Rosamond LN, et al. Sustainable development of the palm oil sector in the Congo Basin: The need for a regional strategy involving smallholders and informal markets. In: CIFOR Infobriefs, No. 255. 2019

[57] RSPO. Principles and Criteria for the Production of Sustainable Palm Oil. Kuala Lumpur: Roundtable on Sustainable Palm Oil; 2018. Available from: https://rspo.org/resources/certification/rspo-principles-criteria-certification

[58] Tropical Forest Alliance. TFA Africa Palm Oil Initiative 5th Regional Meeting. 2018. Available from: https://www.tropicalforestalliance.org/en/news-and-events/news/tfa-2020-africa-palm-oil-initiative-5th-regional-meeting [Accessed: November 2023]

[59] Mobateli A. Congo-Kinshasa: Le pays va relancer plus de 2.000 plantations zaïrianisées et abandonnées. Le Potentiel. 2013. Available from: https://fr.allafrica.com/stories/201302090400.html

[60] Paterson RRM, Lima N. Climate change affecting oil palm agronomy, and oil palm cultivation increasing climate change, require amelioration. Ecology and Evolution. 2018;**8**:452-461. DOI: 10.1002/ece3.3610

[61] Paterson RRM, Kumar L, Shabani F, Lima N. World climate suitability projections to 2050 and 2100 for growing oil palm. Journal of Agricultural Science. 2017;**155**:689-702. DOI: 10.1017/S0021859616000605

[62] Paterson RRM. Longitudinal trends of future climate change and oil palm growth: empirical evidence for tropical Africa. Environmental Science and Pollution Research. 2021;**28**:21193-21203. DOI: 10.1007/s11356-020-12072-5

[63] Seng T-Y, Mohamed Saad SH, Chin C-W, Ting N-C, Harminder Singh RS, Qamaruz Zaman F, et al. Genetic linkage map of a high yielding FELDA Deli×Yangambi oil palm cross. PLoS ONE. 2011;**6**(11):e26593. DOI: 10.1371/journal.pone.0026593

[64] UNFPA. 2023. Available from: https://www.unfpa.org/data/world-population/CD [Accessed: November 2023]

[65] Macrotrends. 2023. Available from: https://www.macrotrends.net/countries/COD/democratic-republic-of-congo/unemployment-rate [Accessed: November 2023]

[66] ALIGN 2023. Available from: https://align-tool.com/source-map/congo-dem-rep#footnote-pimcore_editable_wage-and-income_1_content_textarea-1

[67] Statista. Gross Monthly Minimum Wage in Africa as of 2022, by Country (in U.S. dollars). 2023. Available from: https://www.statista.com/statistics/1262632/gross-monthly-minimum-wage-in-africa-by-country/

[68] Skrine. Minimum wage throughout Malaysia aligned from 1 July 2023. 2023. Available from: https://www.skrine.com/insights/alerts/july-2023/minimum-wage-throughout-malaysia-aligned-from-1-ju

[69] ASEAN Briefing. 2023. Available from: https://www.aseanbriefing.com/doing-business-guide/indonesia/human-resources-and-payroll/minimum-wage

[70] Shahbandeh M. DR Congo: Palm Oil Consumption 2002-2022. 2023. Available from: https://www.statista.com/statistics/489310/palm-oil-consumption-congo/

[71] USDA AS. Palm Oil Explorer. 2023. Available from: https://ipad.fas.usda.gov/cropexplorer/cropview/commodityView.aspx?startrow=11&cropid=4243000&sel_year=2023&rankby=Production [Accessed: November 2023]

[72] FEWSNET. Democratic Republic of Congo Price Bulletin. 2022. Available from: https://www.google.com/url?sa=t&rct=j&q=&esrc=s&source=web&cd=&cad=rja&uact=8&ved=2ahUKEwjz85_7tt-CAxW5UUEAHUKGCR0QFnoECBQQAQ&url=https%3A%2F%2Freliefweb.int%2Freport%2Fdemocratic-republic-congo%2Fdemocratic-republic-congo-price-bulletin-july-2022&usg=AOvVaw2oWWZYFu838ue2MS4E2XEd&opi=89978449

[73] Nordin I, Radzi F, Kumar KS. Sub-Sahara Africa: Palm oil opportunities. OFI July/August. 2021. pp. 26-30. Available from: https://www.google.com/url?sa=t&rct=j&q=&esrc=s&source=web&cd=&cad=rja&uact=8&ved=2ahUKEwivxoe3md-CAxXNYEEAHQVaCFQQFnoECA4QAw&url=https%3A%2F%2Fwww.ofimagazine.com%2Fcontent-images%2Fnews%2FSub-Saharan-Africa_2022-06-28-134655_aaqz.pdf&usg=AOvVaw2x1fGKvw9ubrR_vLIJQD0g&opi=89978449

[74] Radio Okapi. Zone de libre-échange: la RDC appelée à « restructurer son système économique. 2021. Available from: https://www.radiookapi.net/2021/01/02/actualite/politique/zone-de-libre-echange-la-rdc-appelee-restructurer-son-systeme

[75] Pirker J, Mosnier A, Toth G, Giustarini L, Austin KG, Peuser O. Zero Deforestation Palm Oil from Malaysia: The Ferrero Experience. ETFRN News 58; 2017. Available from: www.google.com/url?sa=t&rct=j&q=&esrc=s&source=web&cd=& cad=rja&uact=8&ved=2ahUKEwikzYDCkZqDAxVNS0EAHbrwDZ0QFnoECAoQAQ&url=https%3A%2F%2Fcore.ac.uk%2Fdownload%2Fpdf%2F83641797.pdf&usg=AOvVaw0JXen0NdW8lBx5ZsF1SteS&opi=89978449

[76] Pirker J, Mosnier A, Kraxner F, Havlík P, Obersteiner M. What are the limits to oil palm expansion. Global Environmental Change. 2016;**40**:73-81

[77] Gunarso P, Hartoyo ME, Agus F, Killen TJ. Oil Palm and Land Use Change in Indonesia. Malaysia and Papua New Guinea. In: Reports from the Technical Panels of the 2nd Greenhouse Gas Working Group of the Round table on Sustainable Palm Oil (RSPO), Kuala Lumpur, Malaysia; 2013. Available from: www.google.com/url?sa=t&rct=j&q=&esrc=s&source=web&cd=&c ad=rja&uact=8&ved=2ahUKEwjpgvDdkpqDAxXEWUEAHbR4B0wQFnoECBYQAQ&url=https%3A%2F%2Fwww.tropenbos.org%2Ffile.php%2F1343%2F4_oil_palm_and_land_use_change_gunarso_et_al.pdf&usg=AOvVaw3vXjC8z4H_I4FhVdvIt75P&opi=89978449

[78] Koh L, Miettinen J, Liew SC, Ghazoul J. Remotely sensed evidence of tropical peatland conversion to oil palm. Proceedings of the National Academy of Sciences of the United States of America. 2011;**108**:5127-5132. DOI: 10.1073/pnas.1018776108

[79] Carlson K, Curran L, Asner G, Pittman A, Trigg S, Adeney J. Carbon

emissions from forest conversion by Kalimantan oil palm plantations. Nature Climate Change. 2012;**3**. DOI: 10.1038/NCLIMATE1702. Miettinen et al., Macmillan Publishers Limited; 2012

[80] Schrier-Uij AP, Silvius M, Parish F, Lim KH, Rosediana S, Anshari G. Environmental and social impact of oil palm cultivation on tropical peat. In: Reports from the Technical Panels of the 2nd Greenhouse Gas Working Group of the Roundtable for Sustainable (RSPO). 2013. Available from: https://www.researchgate.net/publication/260058806_Environmental_and_Social_Impacts_of_Oil_Palm_Cultivation_on_Tropical_Peat_-_A_Scientific_Review/figures?lo=1

[81] Miettinen J, Shi C, Liew SC. Two decades of destruction in Southeast Asia's peat swamp forests. Frontiers in Ecology and the Environment. 2012;**10**:124-128. DOI: 10.2307/41480671

[82] Asian Argi. The Benefits of Palm Oil. 2023. Available from: https://www.asianagri.com/en/media-publications/articles/the-benefits-of-palm-oil/

[83] Voora V, Bermúdez S, Farrell JJ, Larrea C, Luna E. Global Market Report: Palm Oil Prices and Sustainability. 2023. Available from: https://www.iisd.org/system/files/2023-06/2023-global-market-report-palm-oil.pdf

[84] Popkin M, Reiss-Woolever VJ, Turner EC, Luke SH. A systematic map of within plantation oil palm management practices reveals a rapidly growing but patchy evidence base. PLOS Sustain Transform. 2022;**1**(7):e0000023. DOI: 10.1371/journal.pstr.0000023

[85] Weng CK. Best-developed practices and sustainable development of the palm oil industry. Journal of Oil Palm Research. 2005;**17**:124-135. Available from: http://jopr.mpob.gov.my/best-developed-practices-and-sustainable-development-of-the-oil-palm-industry/

[86] Tan XJ, Cheor WL, Yeo KS, Leow WZ. Expert systems in oil palm precision agriculture: A decade systematic review. Journal of King Saud University-Computer and Information Sciences. 2022;**34**(4):1569-1594. DOI: 10.1016/j.jksuci.2022.02.006

[87] Chong KL, Kanniah KD, Pohl C, Tan KP. A review of remote sensing applications for oil palm studies. Geo-spatial Information Science. 2017;**20**(2):184-200. DOI: 10.1080/10095020.2017.1337317

[88] Intergovernmental Panel on Climate Change (IPCC). Global Warming of 1.5°C. An IPCC Special Report on the Impacts of Global Warming of 1.5°C above Pre-industrial Levels and Related Global Greenhouse Gas Emission Pathways, in the Context of Strengthening the Global Response to the Threat of Climate Change, Sustainable Development, and Efforts to Eradicate Poverty. Cambridge, UK: Cambridge University Press; 2022. DOI: 10.1017/9781009157940

[89] Svatoňová T, Herak D, Kabutey A. Financial profitability and sensitivity analysis of palm oil plantation in Indonesia. Acta Universitatis Agriculturae et Silviculturae Mendelianae Brunensis. 2015;**63**:1365-1373. DOI: 10.11118/actaun201563041365

[90] Lawder D. World Bank's IFC Proposes Return to Palm Oil Financing in Gabon. 2023. Available from: https://www.reuters.com/article/worldbank-palmoil-idAFL1N39D3T6/

[91] Sinha S, Miller H, DeHaven L, Schulz M. The Intersection of

Agricultural and Financial Markets. Nathan Associates London Ltd; 2015. Available from: www.nathaninc.com

[92] Odhiambo W. Financing african agriculture: Issues and challenges. In: Draft paper to be presented at the Second African Economic Conference at the United Nations Conference Centre (UNCC); Addis Ababa, Ethiopia; 15-17 November 2007. 2007. Available from: https://www.google.com/url?sa=t&rct=j&q=&esrc=s&source=web&cd=&cad=rja&uact=8&ved=2ahUKEwiVjJyi-uGCAxV2WEEAHcWeDvk4ChAWegQIBhAB&url=https%3A%2F%2Fwww.afdb.org%2Ffileadmin%2Fuploads%2Fafdb%2FDocuments%2FKnowledge%2F25120395-FR-ISSUES-AND-CHALLENGES-IN-FINANCIN-FINAL.PDF&usg=AOvVaw00-B0X74tgxhiTXE8if76f&opi=89978449

Chapter 5

Deforestation-Free Palm Oil in Honduras: Challenges, Needs, and Opportunities

Flavio Linares

Abstract

Honduras is the third oil palm production country in Latin America region after Colombia and Guatemala. Deforestation of tropical forest has been key issue for market demand and EU countries, especially now that the new EU regulation has been approved to follow due diligence for export products. In this context, in 2017 a multi-stakeholder platform was integrated by Governmental agencies, private and cooperatives of farmers, and federation and civil society organizations to work together in the Volunteer Agreement for Zero Deforestation. The pause of the COVID 19 and the election of the new government in Honduras slowed down the process of the Voluntary Agreement. The progress achieved and the challenges and opportunities of this Agreement are explained step-by-step and constitute a road map to accelerate compliance with the agreement and therefor, the new regulation of the European Union-EUDR. Honduras palm oil growers and industry aspire to genuine sustainability that is inclusive and empowers people to generate prosperity for themselves and their communities, through production systems that are in balance with nature. The author led the multi-stakeholder plataform for Zero Deforestation in Honduras and Guatemala too.

Keywords: oil palm deforestation, EUDR regulation, oil palm smallholders, Honduras Volunteer Agreement for Zero Deforestation in oil palm sector, challenges and opportunities in the EUDR compliance, multi stakeholder platform, sustainability, inclusive business

1. Introduction

Palm oil is one of the most popular and widely consumed oils; its versatility and oleo chemistry is found in food products, concentrates, cosmetics, cleaning and sanitation products, detergents, biofuels, vitamins, and so on. Its production efficiency is ten times higher in productivity per area than its closest relative, soybeans. The current global production is 79,464 (1000 MT) [1], and by 2050, it will be 90–156 (1000 MT). Its popularity is reflected by its presence in more than 50% of typical items in supermarkets [2]. In the present decade, deforestation and degradation of soils as well as ecosystems have gained enormous importance in value chains. The loss of forests and their degradation has an impact on the loss of biodiversity and carbon.

The resonance has been greater in consumer countries with increasingly strict regulations and markets with a high appetite for raw materials and, to some extent, due to the commitments in the Nationally Determined Contribution—NDC—of producer countries that present very limited capabilities in secondary transformation. Governance undoubtedly affect the implementation of zero-deforestation policies in each value chain and compliance with the New European Deforestation Regulation, approved in June 2023 [3] for producing and exporting countries that will enter into effective December 30, 2024 (EUDR in English).

For more than a decade, we have observed in several countries, and Honduras is no exception, that the production of palm oil has improved the living standards of many farmers, but it has also been associated with innumerable risks such as deforestation, climate change, the loss of biodiversity, conflicts with the use and possession of the land and labor problems depending on the country, the farmer's associativity, and the configurations of organizations and companies [4].

2. Structure of the oil palm agroindustry in Honduras

Oil palm was introduced to Honduras approximately 100 years ago, beginning with 6.5 ha in 1929 by United Brands-UFcO [5]. According to recent studies, there are currently 202,000 cultivated hectares, mainly on the northern coast, in the departments of Atlántida, Cortés, Colón, and Yoro (**Figure 1**). The impact of hurricanes ETA and IOTA caused the loss of approximately 18,000 ha [6]. In Latin America, Honduras ranks third in the Americas, after Guatemala and Colombia in cultivated area with oil palm (**Figure 2**).

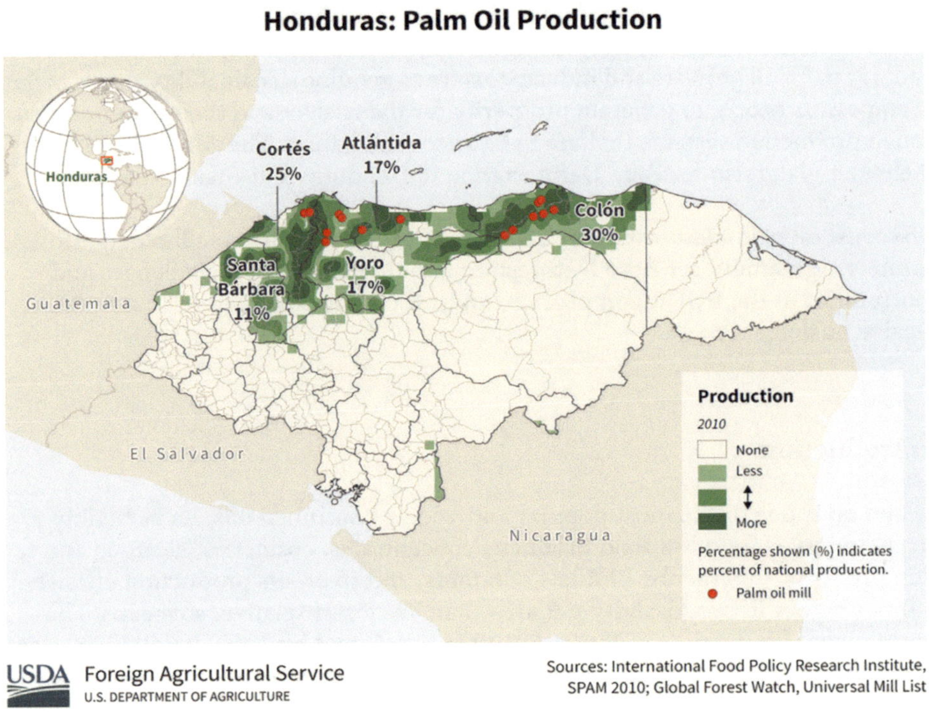

Figure 1.
Oil palm geographic distribution in Honduras.

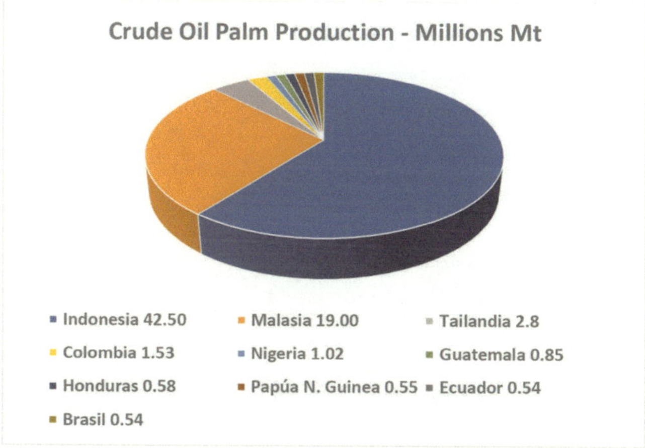

Figure 2.
Honduras in the global top ten of palm oil-producing countries.

Figure 3.
Worker women picking oil palm fresh fruits. HonduCaribe, social company.

Fresh fruit production is concentrated along the Atlantic Coast in the eastern part of the country, with plantations in 41 municipalities. More than 60% of the cultivated area is managed by small producers with extensions ranging from 1 to 25 hectares, so the supply base to the processing plants is in the hands of more than 16,000 small producers. The industry has 15 mills (5 refineries) of which 10 belong to companies in the social sector of the economy (social model based on national law, [7]) and only 5 to private companies. 10% of oil palm farms are managed directly by women and 90% by men.

3. Palm oil, engine of the Honduras national economy

Honduras produced 600,000 MT of palm oil in 2021–2022 [8, 9] with internal consumption of 40%. Globally, it ranks ninth in producing countries (**Figure 2**). The most

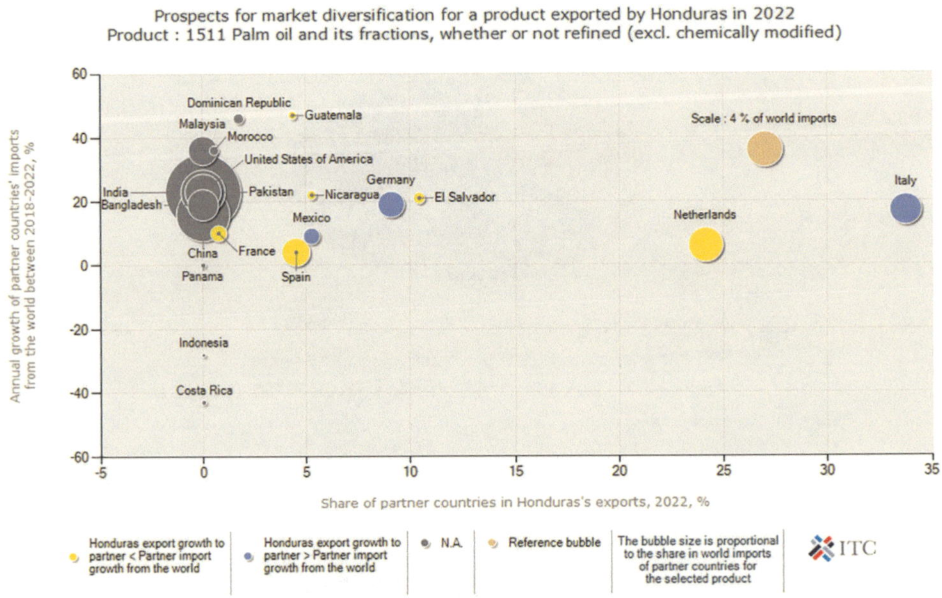

Figure 4.
Trading partner countries for the export of palm oil from Honduras (2022).

important destination is the European Union (**Figures 3** and **4**), which received 83 percent of exports in 2022 [10], while the neighboring countries of Central America and Mexico accounted for the rest. With an export value of USD 400 million, the oilseed crop is an essential foreign exchange generator for Honduras, after coffee [11]. It contributes 3% of the GDP and generates around 33,666 direct jobs and more than 168,330 indirect jobs. The demand for certified oil comes from Western countries.

4. Deforestation and environmental degradation associated with oil palm cultivation in Honduras

Honduras has an area of 112,492 square kilometers with a forest cover of 56%. Unfortunately, Honduras has seen a notable loss of forest cover over the years, with high levels of deforestation driven largely by unsustainable agriculture and illegal logging. On top of this, climate-related hazards such as forest fires, pests, and disease, illegal logging, firewood consumption, and land grabbing have also been enormously damaging. It is estimated that from 1990 to 2020, the country lost 9% of its forest coverage [12]. In 2022, 54.4 kha of natural forest were lost, equivalent 29.3. Mt. of CO2 emissions (Global [13]). From 2002 to 2022, Honduras lost 465,000 ha of primary humid forest, which represents 37% loss of total forest cover in the same period of time. The total area of primary humid forest in Honduras decreased by 22% in this period of time, reports Forest Watch. The protected areas, according to the National Institute of Forest Conservation and Development, Protected Areas and Wildlife—ICF— and Mongabay [14], are being affected by population growth, illegal logging, commercialization of fauna, and planting of monocultures. In the Punta Izopo and Jeanette Kawas national parks, the palm has taken over between 20 and 30% of the protected areas, respectively.

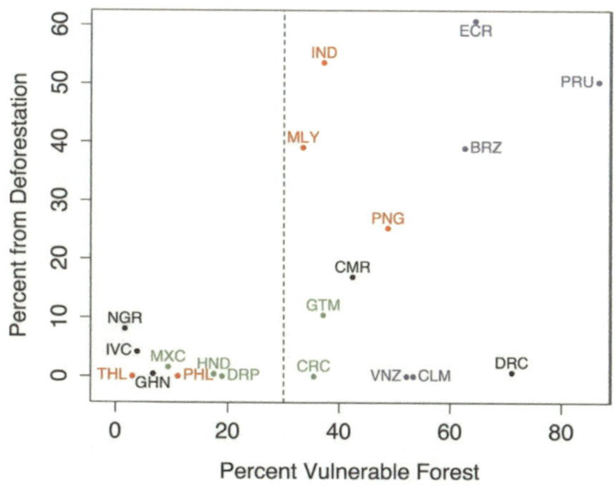

Figure 5.
Vulnerability of high conservation value areas to oil palm expansion in palm oil-producing countries. Source: [15].

The Oil palm expansion in Latin America [15] is following a different land-use change trajectory than the widespread deforestation associated with this industry in Southeast Asia. Deforestation associated with palm in the country from 1989 to 2013 is 0.4% according to studies by Vijay et al. [16]. Although is evident the change in land use in Honduras, from bananas (mostly affected by low prices in 2000) or conversion of pastures to oil palm, there is a high vulnerability of protected areas, wetlands, and riparian zones due to spatial expansion of this crop and violations of legal framework. Vulnerability to forests and areas of high conservation value persists with levels of 18% as a consequence of previous deforestation (**Figure 5**).

The environmental foundation PROLANSATE [17], co-administrator of the national parks Janeth Kawas and Punta Izopo, has alerted citizens to the threats to natural heritage, indicating "the progressive actions of intruders are worrisome, first deforestation and filling of wetlands, then cattle ranching, until they fulfill their ultimate purpose of cultivating oil palm. They drain lagoons, rivers and swamps until they are dry. In some protected areas, the palm was planted before its declaration, however, every year they expand, endangering the core area. In the Punta Izopo and Jeanette Kawas national parks, the African palm has taken over between 20 and 30% of the protected areas, respectively [18].

According to the study carried out by Fundación Solidaridad Latinoamericana (2019) and similar to the studies reported by the ICF, 15,855.22 ha of oil palm are located in buffer zones of protected areas (mainly in Janneth Kawas, Punta Izopo, Punta Sal, and Nombre de Dios) and 129.61 ha in watersheds [19].

In recent years, the Palm Sector has initiated a change of mentality and has listened to the proposal of the Solidaridad experts, in order to invest in vertical growth with high productivity and commitment to the conservation of biodiversity and human rights than to practice a horizontal expansion of the crop (see Solidaridad, Oil Palm Barometer [20]).

5. When the palms speak: Good practices to increase yields per area are key to avoiding expansion

The different Latin American countries show considerable variations in the productivity of palm oil [21]. The highest yield is registered by Guatemala [22] with an

Figure 6.
Salama smallholders cooperative oil palm landscape and riparian zones. Aguan river basin.

average crude oil of 5.6 MT/hectare (ha). In the medium range, Colombia, Costa Rica, Brazil, and Honduras register average yields between 3.4 and 3.0 MT/ha, while Mexico, Peru, and Ecuador register low yields of 2.6 to 2.5 MT/ha. By comparison, Indonesia and Malaysia achieved average yields of 3.6 MT/ha. The yields are influenced by internal factors such as the selection of the planting place, the quality of the genetic material, the seedlings, the age of the plantation, nutrition, maintenance, measurement of growth rates, installed technical capacities (producers or technicians), available resources, and the influence of external factors such as edapho-climatic conditions or recurring climatic variations or as a consequence of climate change.

In countries with a large number of small farmers, there are clear trends, in which lower yields are recorded. The yield of bunches of fresh fruit-RFF in Honduras at the small producer level is 12 MT/ha and 17 MT/ha at the national level (**Figure 6**).

6. Launch of the sustainable production of palm oil project in Honduras-(PASH in Spanish)

In the 2013–2017 period, the Solidaridad Foundation implemented the PASH Project with the objective of promoting the adoption of best sustainable environmental, social, labor, and agricultural practices and achieving RSPO certification. One of the most significant results of this effort was the establishment of the Honduran multi-stakeholder consortium PASH, with a very active membership that included more than 90% of the Honduran palm oil industry, as well as local and international civil society organizations, the Ministry of Agriculture and Livestock (SAG), and local municipal authorities of oil palm-producing areas (Ulua, Aguan, and Chamelecon river basins). The national interpretation of the RSPO standard in the national regulatory framework in 2015 [23] increased capacities of technical teams of key actors and commitments toward the production of certified sustainable palm industrial plants and their supply base. Solidaridad's leadership created frameworks of trust and credibility to guide the Sector toward solid paths of sustainability, closing environmental, social, and productive gaps. Likewise, through professional and expert teams, it provided advice to SAG to support vertical growth rather than horizontal expansion.

7. Management and commitments of the voluntary agreement of zero deforestation of the palm sector of Honduras—AVCD

The Zero Deforestation Voluntary Agreement was generated by the consensual importance of actors in 2017–2018, finalizing its creation in July 2019, with the signature of all interested parties (social and private companies, civil society and state institutions, and the public declaration of commitment [24]. It is the result of the integrated management of the Sustainable Landscape promoted by the Solidaridad Foundation, implementing the baseline of the productive landscape of the northern coast of Honduras. The mapping of the vegetation cover and the main variables that influence or affect the oil palm productive chain deciphered the challenges and the definition of nine interventions aligned to the United Nations Sustainable Development Goals—OSD—(including OSD 15, 13, 2) linked to the protection and conservation of terrestrial ecosystems (**Figures** 7 and **8**). The AVCD agreement was ratified by all stakeholders on October, 2021 [25].

Figure 7.
HONDUPALMA mill: Social company responsible for collecting and industrializing fresh fruit bunches from 28 cooperatives of small producers in the supply chain.

Figure 8.
View of CA-13 main road Honduras divided by oil palm plantations: Jaremar Group and Agroindustrial Corporation Group-CORAPSA.

Figure 9.
Smallholders selling oil palm fresh fruits bunches. Baracoa, Cortes, Honduras.

A jurisdictional landscape model was built in which deforestation, soil loss, water and food security, migration, low productivity, investment in renewable energy, and financing for small producers, among others, were highlighted as challenges. In the multi-stakeholder platform, the findings and prioritization of strategic impact investments [26] were shared, as well as individual dialogs with companies and civil society, explaining three management scenarios: 1. Business as usual (BAS business as usual in English), 2. Businesses with certification standards, and 3. Businesses with an integrated Landscape management approach. In scenario 2, workshops and discussion groups were held to accelerate the adoption of the RSPO and ISSC standard by analyzing win-win, company-community-government business models and an analysis for the RSPO jurisdictional certification option.

Since 2013, it is evident that small producers are forced to be more competitive because the requirements of large buyers in terms of quality, reliability in delivery, and product differentiation have raised the level of competition required. The New European Regulation for the import of deforestation-free products-EUDR, [3] will impact the weakest part of the value chain, small producers, who require greater support and technical, financial, and legal assistance (**Figure 9**).

7.1 Methodological framework

- *Governance*: Founded on the principles of dialog, transparency, and goodwill, a multi-stakeholder platform was established to address the economic, social, and environmental importance of the oil palm value chain, taking advantage of Organización Solidaridad's previous links with the different key stakeholders. The individual and collective discussion, and the leadership to guide the Palm Sector to a Sector and Country management, involved dedication, motivation, and empathy, recognizing the representativeness of the parties and the interpretation of their voices to propose a Voluntary Agreement aligned and respecting the regulatory framework of the country as well as the interpretation of market trends toward obtaining palm oil free from deforestation and exploitation or abuse of related human rights. The approach included discussions about the risks associated with environmental, social, and economic issues and the future consequences with possible changes in consumer demand, fines, and sanctions by the government due to the implementation of deficient practices by

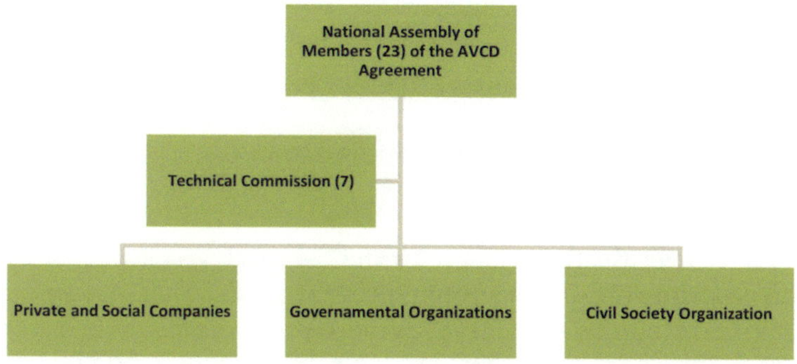

Figure 10.
Organizational chart of the technical Commission of the Voluntary Agreement on zero deforestation of the Honduran palm Oil chain.

producers, intermediaries, and plants of benefit. Governance as a mechanism for work and dialog was made possible by the authentic leadership of Solidaridad staff committed to change. Countless face-to-face and team work sessions were key to reaching consensus between the parties, establishing responsibilities and an ad hoc Technical Commission supported through an assembly election process for the entire sector (see **Figure 10**).

Within the framework of the AVCD Agreement, current legislation and market demands for sustainable palm oil, free of deforestation declarations, were considered such as the Declaration of New York 2014 [27], Amsterdam [28], the buyer's policies No Deforestation, and No burning and No exploitation of communities and workers—NDPE.

The Technical Commission has played a crucial role in the implementation of the AVCD Agreement in response to the mandate established in the Assembly of the companies and governmental and nongovernmental organizations that sign the Agreement. Peter Ducker's phrase "*The best way to predict the future is to create it*" was introduced by Flavio Linares to facilitate and motivate consortium partners and the Technical Commission members.

- *Role of the Technical Commission of the AVCD Agreement*: It is responsible for reviewing, planning, operating, communicating, and socializing the lines of action of the Agreement, using local resources and the experience of Solidaridad Foundation. Fostering due diligence for the geolocation of the oil palm plantations of small, medium and large producers. Analyze of land titles types, history of the crop and the farm, genetic materials, and so on. Request financial resources that can be contributed by donors, market corporations, farmers cooperatives, private and social companies and the government.

- In an assembly of the entire palm sector that signed the AVCD Agreement, the permanent Technical Commission was established by mandate, made up of: FENAPALMAH (Presidency), HONDUPALMA (Vice Presidency), ICF (Secretary), PROLANSATE Foundation (Vocal Prosecutor I), FUCSA Foundation, SOLIDARIDAD (Treasury and Communication), AND ASAPALSA (Member II).

- Objectives of the AVCD agreement
    - o Ensure environmental conservation for present and future generations
    - o Demonstrate the traceability of deforestation-free palm oil production in all processing companies in Honduras
    - o Establish a verification system for the Zero Deforestation process associated with oil palm with a robust monitoring and follow-up system.
    - o Provide differentiated export products, generating trust among customers, mainly in the European market.
- Data collection, information organization, georeferencing, and verification in the Forest Information and Monitoring System—SIGMOF.

The technical Commission, in accordance with the strategy shared in the Assembly of the signatories of the agreement, establishes the steps for the organization of information, analysis, and monitoring using the SIGMOF system, which is the tool used by the ICF Institute for monitoring deforestation, reforestation, and monitoring and control of forest fires in the Republic of Honduras.

A database of each company in the social sector of the economy, private, associations, and cooperatives of producers, was prepared and socialized by the Technical Commission. All the technical teams of the production units, including the members of the National Federation of African Palm Associations of Honduras—FENAPALMAH—were trained on the SIGMOF platform and the information required to upload it to the digital system. Each organization has an access code to the SIGMOF system, protecting the information and data based on strategy shared with all companies and interested parties (see **Figures 11** and **12**).

The strategy focuses on four phases:.

Figure 11.
Strategy and phases to get information from smallholders and companies.

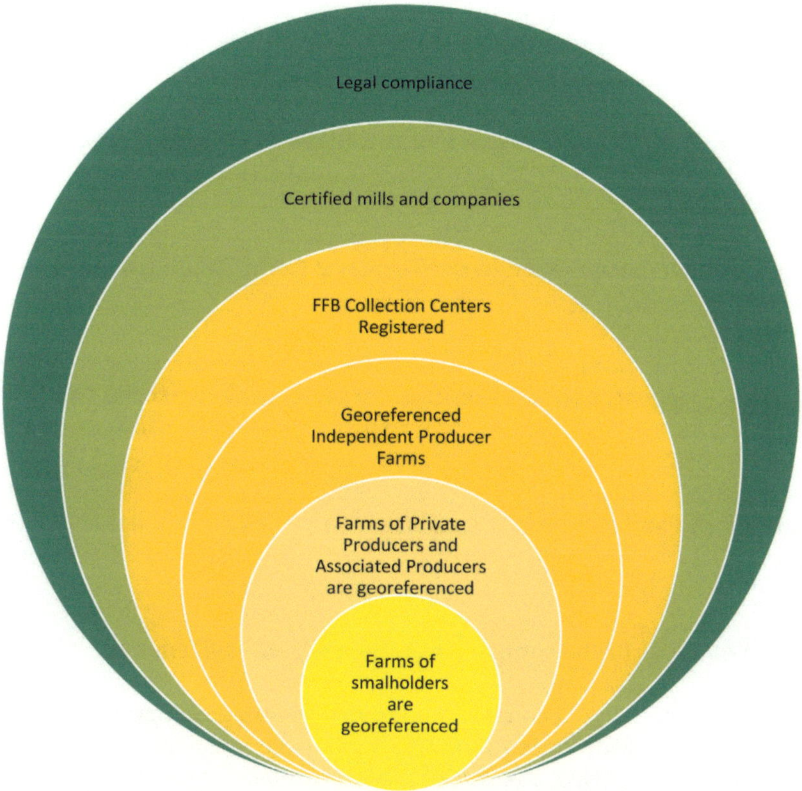

Figure 12.
Work blocks based on the strategy of the AVCD agreement.

a. Benefits of the AVCD agreement

- Contributes tangibly to compliance with the New European Regulation launched in May 2023 by ensuring the conservation of natural resources, producing differentiated palm oil that generates trust in customers in the global market, the traceability of fresh fruit, and the implementation of a compensation system for deforested areas or loss of forest cover.

  - The AVCD Agreement generates inclusive benefits and market opening, financing opportunity, and actions toward the conservation and protection of natural capital, continuous improvement in sustainability processes, job creation, and contribution to the improvement of the livelihoods of the small, medium, and large producers in the palm oil value chain [29].

  - Strengthens the internal control system of the supply base of the processing plants and the strategic investment plans to implement international certification schemes and compliance with national and international regulations.

  - Generates positive synergy and integration of the palm sector with shared responsibility to implement integral solutions in its implementation.

- Contributes directly to the sustainability of the value chain and generation of job opportunities by reducing the irregular migration of Hondurans to the United States of America.

7.2 Results of the AVCD agreement and influence of external factors

7.2.1 Progress results

- Functional governance through the Technical Commission balanced with interested parties.

- Road map for the implementation of the Agreement with iterative phases: Governance, registration, and verification of plantations (social and private companies, independent producers), registration of plantations of small producers, fruit traceability, and registration of intermediaries.

- Definition and structure of the baseline socialized with key stakeholders

- Generation and implementation of monitoring system

- Training of 100% of the companies on the SIGMOF system tool

- 60,000 georeferenced hectares linked to the Information System for Forest Management and Monitoring (SIGMOF), equivalent to 46% of all companies and sustained work in 54% of the rest of the companies.

- Traceability formats and bases for the digital application

- Communication and high collaboration of social and private companies, the National Federation of African Palm Associations of Honduras (FENAPALMAH), environmental and social NGOs, and binding institutions

- Credibility in the system and the broad support of the ministries, the National Institute for Forest Conservation and Development (ICF), Mi Ambiente, and the Secretariat of Agriculture and Livestock (SAG).

- Identification of oil palm plantations in buffer zones and/or protected areas.

7.2.2 External factors

1. Covid 19 Pandemic: The impact of the pandemic in Honduras caused a long pause in the management of the AVCD Agreement due to the protection and control measures established by the government and those implemented by each company and producer cooperative. The physical meetings of the Technical Commission were suppressed and virtual meetings began.

2. Hurricanes ETA and IOTA: In October and November, two meteorological phenomena impacted the north coast, causing historic floods and the loss of 18,000 ha of oil palm and more than 1800 ha of bananas [30], destruction of roads, productive and economic infrastructure with damage around of 0.8

Figure 13.
Fresh fruit transportation system used by smallholders.

percentage points in the national GDP for 2020 and 0.3 percentage points in 2021 [6]. The rehabilitation of planning and industry required more than 6 months, and it was necessary to negotiate with financial organizations and future markets, rescheduling deliveries of crude palm oil. The livelihoods of the rural population of the north coast were devastated by this climatic shock, which caused a pause to the meetings on the AVCD agreement.

3. Conflicts due to invasions of productive units. As of 2022, the agrarian conflict increased and around 21,000 ha productive areas have been invaded by various groups. 80% of this area corresponds to oil palm plantations according to a report from the Honduran Council of Private Enterprise [31].

4. Changes in government authorities 2022. Government agencies that are binding to the AVCD agreement have undergone transition processes and appointments in the different dependencies with long pauses to learn about and accelerate the Agreement according to signed commitments (**Figure 13**).

7.3 Identified barriers to compliance with the AVCD agreement

See **Table 1**. Summary of barriers for the compliance of Voluntary Zero Deforestation Agreement in the oil palm value chain in Honduran (AVCD is Spanish).

No.	Activities	Barriers	Description
1	Establishment of goals to comply with the Zero Deforestation Agreement	Oil palm companies have not shared the goals of the AVCD Agreement with their supply base or fresh fruit buyers except for four RSPO member companies	Establishment and adequate publication of annual and consolidated goals with the supply base of fresh fruit, highlighting the importance of the agreement in the production and commercialization of palm oil
2	Georeferencing of own palm oil farms of private	Georeferenced and mapped farms. Five companies must	The technical staff of all the companies have been trained on how to order the

No.	Activities	Barriers	Description
	and social companies with legal documentation and provision of information to the SIGMOF system (Forest Information and Monitoring System)	upload the information to the SIGMOF Monitoring and Evaluation system	information and upload it to the SIGMOF system. It will require a reinforcement in the knowledge given to changes of personnel in the companies.
3	"Zero-deforestation Policies" must be socialized in the fresh fruit bunch (FFB) supply chain.	Few companies have Zero Deforestation policies; others require improvements in line with the signed Zero Deforestation Agreement, the NDPE policy for buyers, and the new European Union regulations	Zero deforestation policies must be updated and disclosed to all staff and to fresh fruit suppliers and stakeholders in an appropriate manner.
4	Analysis of business risks associated with deforestation or degradation of ecosystems	There is risk analysis in companies certified with the RSPO, ISCC, RA standards. However, at the level of groups or small holders' cooperatives, there is no risk analysis and possibly no information on the commitments acquired by palm oil mills.	The risk analysis matrix must be part of the annual operating plan of the mills, companies, and smallholders cooperatives. Mills must publish the risks incurred when acquiring fresh fruit bunches from dubious origin; in the same way, smallholders and independent producers must understand the Zero Deforestation Agreement signed by companies, FENAPALMAH members, and so forth as an essential part for the business to be sustainable.
5	Strengthen the Collection Centers for fresh fruit bunches free of deforestation	Absence of education and training programs for those in charge of the Collection Centers for fresh fruit bunches on the sustainability of the oil palm	Companies and mills should invest in education programs emphasizing the sustainability pillars, especially the importance of acquiring FFB with transparency, free from deforestation or from areas unsuitable for cultivation (i.e., areas with slopes greater than 30 degrees)
6	Land-use change evaluation studies—LUCA—by company from the year established in the zero-deforestation agreement AVCD: 2010	The companies (4) certified with the RSPO standard have compensation plans approved by RSPO for their own plantations, while the remaining (11) have not done the LUCA studies. This includes producers in the supply base	The evaluation of land-use change—LUCA—is essential to ensure the location of the farms planted with oil palm and the history of land-use change. Companies must invest in LUCA and share them with the Technical Commission.
7	Update to companies on national regulation and certification standards demanded by the market	There are staff from companies and Producer Associations with limited knowledge of national laws and regulations, RSPO, RA, ISCC certification schemes.	Training program on the National Interpretation of the RSPO standard approved for Honduras by the RSPO Board of Governors in July 2022. Train companies and producers on the business plan to aspire to RSPO Certification. Road map for the implementation of closing certification gaps and external audits where appropriate.

No.	Activities	Barriers	Description
8	Update to companies on the new European Regulation for the importation of palm oil and its deforestation-free derivatives	On June 2023, the European Parliament approved the Regulation on deforestation-free products, which includes palm oil, beef, timber, coffee, cocoa, rubber, and soy. The rules will also apply to a number of derived products, including selected palm oil-based derivatives (used, for example, as components in personal care products), with a review to take place in 2 years to see whether other products should be covered	The due diligence on the origin of the fresh fruit bunches and their processing by the extracting companies that export to the European Union must be documented, especially the RSPO certified product with Mass Balance. Products without documentation and due diligence will not be accepted in the European market due to lack of transparency. It is urgent to integrate the New European Regulation into the strategic plans and annual plans of companies and cooperatives of small, medium and large producers as well as in the work plans of intermediaries and administrators of FFB collection centers.
9	Internal Control System-ICS for production system in the fields, mills and refineries.	Companies certified by international standards (RSPO, ISCC, RA) have an ICS that is reviewed annually. The auditors must consider the national interpretation document of the RSPO standard for Honduras, which includes the legal and international framework and the commitments signed in the Zero Deforestation Voluntary Agreement.	Participatory ICS, definition of responsibilities and budget allocation. Include in the system the managers of the Collection Centers, fresh fruit transporters, leaders of groups of producers (small, medium and large). Share the ICS with the state organizations that sign the agreement
10	Traceability of the origin of the fresh fruit bunches	The Technical Commission has structured a system for use by the signatories of the Agreement. You have reviewed two digital traceability tools. It remains to socialize and adjust the tools depending on the type of provider.	Define the cost of using the tools and advice to companies and smallholders.
11	Land ownership or oil palm farms	Due diligence in land ownership requires: a. Review of the documentation available by the Producer and analysis of the property by the regulatory entity (INA, Property Institute) and b. In special cases of palm in buffer zones or core zones, the competence corresponds to the ICF.	Provide training to small, medium and large producers regarding land legalization protocol prepared by the National Agrarian Institute (INA) and Solidaridad Network (supported by RSPO). Get financial resources to support INA personnel to verify all oil palm plantations locations.
12	Incentives for Producers: Small, medium and large	Limited financial and economic incentives for producers	Most companies punish growers for poor-quality fresh fruit bunches but not for transparency and good quality. It is

No.	Activities	Barriers	Description
			normal that loans are given for the purchase of fertilizers or harvest advances, but not technical assistance that includes the issue of transparency of the origin of the FFB. Engage traders and corporate buyers of sustainable palm oil willing to provide incentives for producers in adherence to their NDPE policies and beyond certification
13	Financing for compliance with the AVCD Agreement and operation of the Technical Commission	The Technical Commission works *ad honorem* with a minimum contribution from the companies. It is necessary that the signatory companies of the agreement contribute resources to finance the signed Agreement and therefore the activities defined in the Budget prepared by the Technical Commission	The Technical Commission has worked hard on a voluntary basis, led by Solidaridad. Economic resources are required to comply with the activities of the Commission and those included in the operating plan defined in the Agreement.
14	Monitoring, Verification, and Reporting System	Review and implement a monitoring and reporting system with evidence that reflects the commitment acquired by the parties that signed the Agreement	Standardize the monitoring, verification, and reporting system at the company level.
15	Communication and public disclosure.	Establish the communication strategy, highlighting the importance of the conservation of natural resources and legal compliance with no deforestation and degradation of natural resources.	Focus communication on two key audiences: Producers of fresh fruit bunches and corporate markets that encourage their active involvement in operations.

Table 1.
Barriers to compliance of the AVCD agreement.

7.4 Opportunities to complement EUDR with the AVCD agreement

See **Table 2**. Summary of opportunities to complement EUDR regulation by the AVCD agreement.

No.	Key actors	Activities	Opportunities
1	Mills and smallholders' cooperatives and independent producers	Establishment of goals to comply with the Zero Deforestation Agreement—AVCD	a. The goals of the companies and producer cooperatives will be aligned with the objectives of the Agreement b. Publish and socialize the targets with the supply base

No.	Key actors	Activities	Opportunities
			and stakeholders in appropriate language and through effective means
2	Mills and smallholders' cooperatives and independent producers	Georeferencing and maps of oil palm farms with the respective legal documentation	a. Verifying location information and legal documentation will enable transparency and trust in oil palm operations b. Establish strategic alliances with INA, ICF, SAG, NGOs
3	Mills, Smallholders' Cooperatives, Technical Commission of the Agreement, Policy advisors.	Zero Deforestation Policies in the supply chain of fresh fruit bunches	a. Highlight the importance of the Zero Deforestation commitment with clear policies and known by all producers at the level of each organized group, private companies, and the social sector of the economy b. Align the zero-deforestation policy with the policies of palm oil traders (NDPE) and the New European Regulation
4	Mills, Smallholders' Cooperatives, Technical Commission of the Agreement, Policy advisors.	Analysis of business risks associated with deforestation or degradation of ecosystems	a. Evaluate the risks with the participation of producers, Boards of Directors of Producer Cooperatives, and binding government agencies. b. Train on risk analysis methodologies and its action plan. c. Complement if possible with satellite images from other sources/verify the findings in the field.
5	Mills, Companies, and Smallholders' Cooperatives	Responsible collection centers using tools for the documentation of FFB from farmers	a. Optimize the collection of information from fresh fruit suppliers b. Keep reliable records of the origin of the fruit (volume and quality) c. Correlate the volume of FFB with the good practices management
6	Companies and Smallholders Cooperatives, ICF, SAG, MI AMBIENTE, Municipalities	Evaluation of land-use change—LUCA—by company/producers from the year 2010 approved and established in the Zero Deforestation Agreement	a. Demonstrate with evidence the change in land use to oil palm. b. Use technical support tools
7	Mills, Companies and Smallholders' Cooperatives	Establish the areas deforested by company or group of producers to define the compensation areas	Socialize the compensation area with government agencies and purchasers of palm oil as well as with certification bodies.

No.	Key actors	Activities	Opportunities
		according to the certification standard or national regulation	
8	Companies and smallholders' cooperatives, Technical Commission. RSPO, ISCC	Update on national regulation and certification standards required by the market	a. Increase the capacities of companies and producers, key government organizations, and civil society on the most demanded certification standards in the market. b. Accompany or advise extracting companies and producers on good practices of international standards
9	Companies, mills and smallholders cooperatives, Technical Commission, Palm oil buyers, donors	Traceability of the origin of the bunches of fresh fruit	a. Provide reliable and credible evidence using robust tools. b. Do pilot tests of the digital tools and database tables and the required adjustments c. Share fruit traceability results with palm oil buyers, government organizations
10	Companies, mills Smallholders cooperatives, Technical Commission, Buyers of palm oil, INA, ICF	Land ownership or oil palm farms	Socialize and train producers on good practices and the INA Land Regularization Protocol in order to advise owners.

Table 2.
Opportunities to promote zero deforestation in oil palm under the AVCD agreement.

Author details

Flavio Linares
Programs for Central America, Mexico and Caribbean Region, Solidaridad Network, Tegucigalpa, Honduras

*Address all correspondence to: flavioflavus@gmail.com

References

[1] Palm Oil Explorer. 2023

[2] Lee HA. Palm oil is in everything, and it's hurting more than the orangutans. EcoWatch. 2019. Available from: https://www.ecowatch.com/palm-oil-environmental-costs-2640781015.html

[3] Forwood G, Connellan C, Killick J, Nordin S. 10 Key Things to Know about the New EU Deforestation Regulation. New York: White and Case Firm; 2023

[4] Fromm I, Ferrer M, Mengel S. Sustainable Palm Oil Production in Honduras: Myth or Reality. Bern University of Applied Sciences, School of Agricultural, Forest and Food Sciences. Switzerland; 2020

[5] World Rainforest Movement. Neocolonialism and Plantations on the Garifuna Coast of Central America. Netherlands: Bulletin 226; 2016

[6] CEPAL. Evaluación de los efectos e impactos causados por la tormenta tropical Eta y el huracán Iota en Honduras. Santiago de Chile; 2022

[7] La Gazeta. Ley y Reglamento del Sector Social de la Economía. 1986

[8] Golden Agri Resources. Agribusiness and Food. Three Things You Should Know about Palm Oil in Latin America. Singapore; 2023

[9] Index Mundi. Palm Oil. Honduras, USA: United States Department of Agriculture; 2023

[10] ITC. Trade Map. Trade Statistics for International Business Development. Import & Export Values, Volumes, Growth Rates, Market Shares. Geneva, Switzerland; 2023

[11] Ficha de Comercio Exterior. Honduras. 2021

[12] Monserrat X. UNDP. How Forest and Young People are Solving Honduras's Water Crisis. New York, USA; 2023

[13] Forest Watch. Honduras. Cover Forest Loss. 2022

[14] Guevara L, Frazier L. Mongabay Latam. Honduras: Palma Africana se apodera del agua y areas protegidas. Lima; 2019

[15] Furumo PR, Mitchell Aide T. Characterizing commercial oil palm expansion in Latin America: Land use change and trade. Environmental Research Letters. 2017

[16] Vijay V, Pimm SL, Jenkins CN, Smith SJ. The impacts of oil palm on recent deforestation and biodiversity loss. PLoS One. 2016;**11**(7):e0159668. DOI: 10.1371/journal.pone.0159668

[17] PROLANSATE. Honduras en sus manos Noticias. Devastación ambiental "Sin Cuarentena" en el Parque Nacional Punta Izopo. Cortés, Honduras; 2020

[18] Guevara L, Frazier L. Honduras: Palma Africana se apodera del agua y de áreas protegidas. Mongabay. 2019

[19] Solidaridad Network. Honduran Palm Oil Sector Commits to Zero Deforestation. Utrecht, The Netherlands; 2019

[20] Solidaridad. Oil Palm Barometer. Utrecht, The Netherlands; 2022

[21] Kuepper B, Drost S, Piotrowski M, Rijk G. Chain Reaction Research. Latin

American Palm Oil Linked to Social Risks, Local Deforestation. Washington, D.C.; 2021

[22] GREPALMA. Guatemala Oil Palm Growers Guild. Sustainable Palm Oil Agroindustry in Guatemala. Guatemala, Central America; 2021

[23] RSPO. Roundtable on Sustainable Palm Oil. National Interpretation of the International RSPO Principles and Criteria of the Republic of Honduras. Kuala Lumpur, Malaysia; 2015

[24] Michail N. Honduras Commits to Deforestation Free Supply Chain. Available from: https://www.foodnavigator-latam.com/Article/2019/07/29/Honduran-palm-oil-sector-commits-to-deforestation-free-supply-chain

[25] Solidaridad Central America. Chain Reaction. Sustainable Palm Oil Production in Honduras. Available from: https://www.solidaridadnetwork.org/news/solidaridad-central-america/

[26] PLB Netherlands Environmental Agency. Eco agriculture, solidaridad. Modelización espacial de escenarios para apoyar la gestión integrada de paisajes en la Costa Caribe del Norte de Honduras: Un estudio de caso sobre las estrategias en el paisaje para alcanzar los Objetivos de Desarrollo Sostenible. 2018

[27] Forest Declaration Assessment. What is the New York Declaration on Forests? New York; 2014

[28] Amsterdam Declaration Partnership. Amsterdam Declaration. Towards Eliminating Deforestation from Agriculture Commodity Chains with European Countries by Undersigned Countries: Germany, Italy, Netherlands. Denmark, France, Norway, United Kingdom, Amsterdam, The Netherlands; 2015

[29] Linares F. Solidaridad Network. Presentación introductoria del Acuerdo Voluntario Cero Deforestacion de Palma Aceitera de Honduras. La Ceiba, Atlántida, Honduras; 2019

[30] Maxwell M. Eurofruit. Honduras Counts Cost of Eta and Iota Hurricanes. London; 2020

[31] COHEP. Prensa. Contenido publicado originalmente bajo licencia CC de atribución. Available from: https://www.laprensa.hn/honduras/honduras-80-las-tierras-invadidas-pais-son-palma-africana-NF13168500. 2023